Understanding Fetal Alcohol
Spectrum Disorder

Understanding Fetal Alcohol Spectrum Disorder

A Guide to FASD for Parents, Carers and Professionals

Maria Catterick and Liam Curran

Foreword by Edward P. Riley PhD

Jessica Kingsley *Publishers*
London and Philadelphia

First published in 2014
by Jessica Kingsley Publishers
73 Collier Street
London N1 9BE, UK
and
400 Market Street, Suite 400
Philadelphia, PA 19106, USA

www.jkp.com

Library of Congress Cataloging in Publication Data
Catterick, Maria.
  Understanding fetal alcohol spectrum disorder : a guide to FASD for parents, carers and professionals /
Maria Catterick and Liam Curran.
    pages cm
  Includes bibliographical references and index.
  ISBN 978-1-84905-394-5 (alk. paper)
  1. Fetal alcohol syndrome. I. Curran, Liam. II. Title.
  RG629.F45C42 2014
  618.3'26861--dc23
                            2014007799

British Library Cataloguing in Publication Data
A CIP catalogue record for this book is available from the British Library

ISBN 978 1 84905 394 5
eISBN 978 0 85700 758 2

Printed and bound in the United States

A special dedication to LJ and LH for all your life lessons, inspiration and smiles.

CONTENTS

FOREWORD

This is a guide that is long overdue. The authors, a social worker and a carer, both with a great deal of experience and understanding of fetal alcohol spectrum disorder, have put together a fabulous resource that provides an easy-to-read guide for individuals dealing with this important issue. I have been studying the effects of prenatal alcohol exposure on brain and behavioral development for over 35 years, and when I began my research in this area, I was sure it would be a short-term project. Research would confirm or not the clinical findings of Dr. Ken Jones and Dr. David Smith in 1973 that alcohol was a teratogen, an agent capable of causing birth defects. If alcohol was established as a teratogen causing birth defects, pregnant women and women considering pregnancy would stop drinking and the problem would be solved.

How naïve I was back then. There is little doubt that within ten years after the identification of fetal alcohol syndrome (FAS) by Jones and Smith, human data, and data collected with animal models clearly established the damaging effects of prenatal alcohol exposure, prompting the US Surgeon General to issue a warning about the hazards of alcohol consumption during pregnancy. But despite another 30 years of research, the warnings, the public debate about alcohol use during pregnancy, the problem remains, and it is indeed a staggering problem, and a preventable one.

Having worked in this field for this long, I regularly hear from parents and caregivers about the problems and issues they face in caring for their children (regardless of their age) who have fetal alcohol spectrum disorder (FASD). I often hear 'I can't get services …no one seems to understand … we received a diagnosis but there is no follow through with service …what will happen to my child when I am no longer able to take care of them.'

This book will certainly help in answering many of these questions. Maria Catterick and Liam Curran have put together a useful guide covering many of the important aspects when one considers FASD, from nicely describing the condition, to the issues of diagnosis and the lifelong implications of these disorders. They conclude with chapters on how to deal with FASD in the numerous systems and places where individuals with an FASD often have contact and how policy and practice need to respond to these conditions. Although there are numerous resources on FASD that are available, this guide does an outstanding job in putting FASD into perspective within a single resource. FASD is a tragic, preventable condition, but it is not a sentence to a life of tragedy and misfortune. Certainly, I have witnessed many sad tales regarding those impacted by prenatal alcohol exposure, but I have also seen lots of cases of individuals, who have met the challenges imposed by their alcohol exposure histories and are leading happy, productive lives.

This guide provides a resource that should help increase the numbers successfully dealing with their challenges and hopefully help prevent the tragic consequences of prenatal alcohol exposure.

Edward P. Riley PhD

Distinguished Professor.

Director, Center for Behavioral Technology

San Diego State University

AUTHORS' NOTE

This book seeks to honour all the extraordinary children, adults and families who are working hard to succeed despite the often daily challenges, lack of awareness and lack of services which abound. Your tenacity of spirit is worthy of gold medals all round. We long for the day when you say to someone that you are a person with FASD or are a caregiver of a child with FASD and you are no longer asked the question, 'What is FASD?'

This book also seeks to honour the professionals and practitioners who have stepped into 'no man's land' to explore what is beyond the limited understanding, limited budgets and existing services, and who have channelled a pathway forwards with creativity, ingenuity and that most excellent of philosophies: simple common sense. Your efforts have changed the lives of numerous families and shored up their foundations, which may at times have felt like sinking sand. Let us go onwards and upwards, as there is much more to do.

> It ought to be remembered that there is nothing more difficult to take in hand, more perilous to conduct, or more uncertain in its success, than to take the lead in the introduction of a new order of things. Because the innovator has for enemies all those who have done well under the old conditions, and lukewarm defenders in those who may do well under the new. This coolness arises partly from fear of the opponents, who have the laws on their side, and partly from the incredulity of men, who do not readily believe in the new things until they have had a long experience of them.
>
> (Machiavelli, *The Prince*, 1513)

INTRODUCTION

This book has been written by a social worker and a foster carer, two roles which are often on the frontlines responding to the complex needs of people living with fetal alcohol spectrum disorder (FASD). It is dearly hoped that parents, carers and professionals alike will find it a useful starting point to gain an understanding of a disability which still goes unseen in many parts of our world today. It will provide insights and ideas about how to support individuals with FASD across their lifespan and raise awareness of the need to protect those who are yet to be born. It should also serve to highlight to professionals engaged in child welfare the need to consider FASD as a critical feature within the common assessment framework due to a high prevalence rate of FASD in the child welfare system (Burd *et al.* 2011; Fuchs *et al.* 2008; Popova *et al.* 2013).

Fetal alcohol spectrum disorder(s) is an umbrella term which is used to describe a range of mental, physical and neurobehavioural birth defects that result from an alcohol-exposed pregnancy. It is one of the leading causes of preventable birth defects and developmental disabilities in the world today. FASD is a permanent brain injury to the developing fetus due to alcohol being a teratogen, which is a substance that disrupts the developing fetus. Alcohol enters the bloodstream of the fetus without any filter or barrier to its journey from the mother's bloodstream, and the toxic elements of alcohol harm the fetus. Alcohol is more dangerous than many of the illicit drugs that are used within society today.

It is important to clarify from the beginning that FASD in itself is not a clinical diagnostic term but merely an umbrella term to encompass a constellation of effects that can occur when alcohol is consumed in pregnancy. These 'effects' vary widely in how they present in children who have been exposed to alcohol in the womb. What is known from the body of research carried out over the past four decades is that FASD is prevalent in our families, schools and foster care and adoption services. Whilst understanding of fetal alcohol exposure has been developing from biblical times, it is only recently that a true understanding of the mechanisms of harm have emerged due to the rapid advances of medical research. FASD can involve a range of malformations, but by far the most significant is permanent organic brain injury. It is now clear that a child exposed to alcohol may have a range of intellectual and behavioural outcomes that remain with them across the complete lifespan.

This range of neurobehavioural conditions is still largely unknown throughout the Western world with the exception of perhaps the US and Canada, both of which have made great strides over the past 15–20 years to alert parents-to-be of the dangers and risks that alcohol poses in pregnancy. One of the conditions under the umbrella term of FASD, namely fetal alcohol syndrome (FAS) which is marked by the physical appearance of craniofacial abnormalities, small head circumference and growth deficiencies and difficulties, is more understood due to the visible nature of the disability. Less well known, however, are the other conditions under the umbrella which leave many children undiagnosed or misdiagnosed due to a lack of awareness of the invisibility of neurobehavioural implications of alcohol exposure. Only seeing FAS as a singular effect of an alcohol-exposed pregnancy, rather than the range of effects along a spectrum, has a huge impact on the individual and the family who may struggle to obtain the correct services and supports which can ameliorate some of the consequences of this exposure. Thousands of studies conducted in many different nations have found that children born of an alcohol-exposed pregnancy can have lifelong disabilities, yet for reasons unknown this vital public health information is still ignored, disputed and even rejected by academics, physicians and politicians. The result of this lack of recognition is an estimated one million children born each year around the world with a neurobehavioural condition that will impact in the home, school and lifespan of the newborn child of a mother who consumed alcohol while pregnant.

It is perhaps somewhat surprising that this book cannot give accurate statistics for how many children are born with an FASD condition. At the current time there is no universal screening for FASD in maternity hospitals, and as such, what an educationalist must depend on are 'estimates' from different parts of the developed world. What can be said for certain is that both the US and Canada have been leading the way in providing an understanding of this disability. The most reliable statistics emerge from various US studies that conclude a figure of 9.1 births per 1000 are affected by prenatal alcohol exposure (PAE). This statistic is most commonly used to give an indication of what might be the level within a general culture. FAS is estimated at 0.2–1.5 cases per 1000 live births. Bertrand *et al.* (2004) noted that such rates are comparable with or above other common developmental disabilities such as Down syndrome or spina bifida. The prevalence rate of FASD may be higher in some settings, with some studies suggesting that the rate in high-risk populations of foster care and adoption may be as high as 10–15 per 1000.

Whilst significant medical advancements have occurred over many years to address ill health, modern hedonistic lifestyles of drug and alcohol use across all spectrums of society can undo that work. The fallout of drug and alcohol use and misuse is one of the greatest challenges to our modern health services. The impact of this destructive activity is considerable across many domains of society including mental health, criminal justice, education and health and social care.

This book addresses the lack of understanding of FASD, and the impact on the individual, family, social services and society, by creating an understanding of how FASD may present across the lifespan and the resulting psychosocial consequences for the individual living with FASD, the caregiver and society in general. There is an exploration of diagnosis and diagnostic techniques which are key to preventing or ameliorating many of the secondary disabilities and identifying the types of support and intervention that practitioners may need to provide across multidisciplinary service provision. Practical tools and insights which can have the effect of stabilising the home, increasing educational attainment, promoting positive community connections and providing a foundation for future success are examined. Finally, the book provides some discussions around the wider practical and policy perspectives utilising insights from frontline workers in various nations and considering public health perspectives to both prevent the condition and lessen the secondary outcomes for those affected by an alcohol-exposed pregnancy.

Professionals in allied health positions as well as parents and carers all have a role in educating society about alcohol harm, and in doing so may prevent future children from being exposed to alcohol during pregnancy. There is a need to bring this disability from the shadows and set it within the context of disability services in our modern health systems throughout the world. Strong and courageous women who have given birth to a child with FASD and were denied this education are now speaking out within communities. They need to be respected, listened to and supported in telling their stories. From the personal accounts of birth mothers, adoptive parents and foster parents, it is without question that FASD needs a multimodal approach within local communities to provide positive futures for children and adults living with this lifelong condition. As a disability, FASD is pervasive within the systems of social services, education, health and justice. There is an urgent need to work collectively and strategically at all levels of society to create prevention policies and provide services for those affected.

Chapter 1

WHAT IS FASD?

BRIEF OVERVIEW

When the development of our central nervous system (CNS) is disturbed or interrupted, we risk developing serious lifelong neurological abnormalities which can impair our sensory systems, movement, control or cognitive functions. This is true for all organisms with a well-developed nervous system. What is known from the body of research presented to date is that alcohol in pregnancy has the ability to disrupt the normal development path of the fetal brain. Alcohol is a toxin and poison. As a substance it is a teratogen, meaning it can move freely from the mother's bloodstream to that of her unborn child and interfere with the development of the fetus.

One might be forgiven for thinking that fetal alcohol spectrum disorder (FASD) is a new phenomenon, or indeed a new classification of a disability, but the advancements in medical science over the past 10–15 years has provided more solid evidence that alcohol consumed during pregnancy can have adverse effects on the developing fetus. Specifically, with such scientific advances of magnetic resonance imaging (MRI) within health care systems, we are now able to see the human brain in more acute detail than ever before. Advanced abilities in the neuroscience of brain scanning can map the way our brains interact with thoughts, words and action. In addition, functional imaging research has demonstrated functional and neurochemical differences in those exposed prenatally to alcohol. Research demonstrates that individuals exposed to alcohol prenatally exhibit 'structural alterations…in brain size, shape, and symmetry' (McGee and Riley 2006). It is this 'science' that is establishing a present cold reality of the historical concern that alcohol, as a toxin, can derail the brain development mechanisms of the unborn child in utero.

The impact of the alcohol exposure leads to a categorisation of harm under the umbrella term fetal alcohol spectrum disorder(s), which is categorised primarily into the following specific areas:

- fetal alcohol syndrome (FAS)

- partial fetal alcohol syndrome (PFAS)

- alcohol-related neurodevelopmental disorder (ARND)

- alcohol-related birth defects (ARBD)

- neurodevelopmental disorder as a result of prenatal exposure to alcohol (ND-PAE).

TERMINOLOGY

The definitions of the aforementioned disorders are as follows:

- *Fetal alcohol spectrum disorder* (FASD). This is used to encompass the individual terms in a collective presentation. FASD as a term acknowledges that this disability is on a continuum which is expressed by the organic brain injury and the corrupted/faulty brain wiring of the CNS. It incorporates all of the presentations of fetal exposure to alcohol while in utero. It is an umbrella term and not a diagnostic one.

- *Fetal alcohol syndrome* (FAS). Fetal death is the most extreme outcome from drinking alcohol during pregnancy. People with FAS might have abnormal facial features, growth problems and CNS problems. CNS damage may present as learning, memory, attention span, communication, vision or hearing issues.

- *Partial fetal alcohol syndrome* (PFAS). PFAS has a confirmed history of PAE but may lack growth deficiency or the complete facial dysmorphology. Central nervous system damage can be present at the same level as FAS. Individuals with PFAS may have all the same CNS deficits as FAS.

- *Alcohol-related neurodevelopmental disorder* (ARND). People with ARND might have intellectual disabilities and problems with behaviour and learning. They might do poorly in school and have difficulties with mathematics, memory, attention, judgement and poor impulse control.

- *Alcohol-related birth defects* (ARBD). People with ARBD might have problems with the heart, kidneys or bones, or with hearing (or a mix of these).

- *Neurodevelopmental disorder as a result of prenatal exposure to alcohol* (ND-PAE). This new term, which will likely take precedence over ARND as we move forward in understanding, has been established as of May 2013 in the fifth edition of the *Diagnostic and Statistical Manual of Mental Disorders*.

Diagnostic processes for FASD are currently conducted utilising four main diagnostic tools developed in the US and Canada. A common thread running through these assessment tools is establishing where alcohol consumed during pregnancy has created a biological injury of the brain. This brain injury can and will present in a variety of ways as the child seeks to make their way in the world. The problem of recognising children who have suffered from an alcohol-exposed pregnancy is that only children with FAS on the spectrum of effects will have outwardly physical effects.

Individuals with FASD may experience difficulties with memory, cognition, executive functioning and adaptive functioning. What is noted in many study findings is that an individual with FASD may have difficulty organising, planning or recalling a sequence of events in time. Typical brain dysfunction in individuals with FASD may be as follows:

- inconsistent memory and recall

- slower and inconsistent cognitive and auditory processing

- co-occurring mental illness(es)

- difficulty in managing/filtering sensory stimuli from the environment

- poor emotional regulation

- low self-esteem

- difficulties in controlling impulsive behaviours

- difficulties in understanding rules and regulations

- poor motor coordination

- sleep and eating disorders

- inability to read social cues or predict outcomes.

What is more concerning perhaps is that this lifelong disability is largely unrecognised within communities, schools, child care services, fostering and in the international field of adoption. It is accepted in the literature and the vast bodies of research outcomes that when FASD is unseen and undiagnosed, the prognosis for these individuals may be poor. The development of secondary disabilities can stem from the 'brain injury' as detailed by Streissguth *et al.* (1996):

- mental health disorders (90%)

- alcohol and drug addiction (60%)

- trouble with the law, incarceration (60%)

- inappropriate sexual behaviours (50%)

- difficulty in employment stability (80%)

- unable to live independently (80%).

All of these impacts are explored within a framework of recognition, screening and diagnosis of FASD. It is important to begin first with considering the history of the disability and the science of alcohol harm to fully understand and recognise the resulting effects on the individual with PAE.

> I will examine more of the 'neglect cases' to include prenatal exposure to alcohol in the lens.
>
> (Alison N, social worker, Dublin, Ireland, 9 May 2013)

Common questions about FASD are:

- *Is FASD curable?* The effects of PAE are irreversible. Individuals with FASD and their families deal with the effects of this disability by managing the resulting behaviours and addressing the medical implications. There is no cure for this particular type of brain injury and the individual will always have this disability.

- *Can it be inherited from a parent who has FASD?* Individual adults with FASD who marry and have children cannot pass on FASD. The science of FASD is that it can only happen once the egg is fertilised by the sperm. From this point on, alcohol consumed by the mother has the potential to harm the developing fetus. There are, however, a number of genetic conditions that 'look like' FASD, and the very nature of genetics tells us that such genetic conditions can be passed from either parent to their offspring.

- *Does FASD apply only to children or adolescents?* FASD is a permanent, lifelong neurological issue that does not improve with age. In fact, it could be argued that the opposite is the case. Behaviours that do not conform to expected norms are viewed more severely when perpetrated by someone who is older than 18 years of age. Society is less forgiving at this stage in life. This is a major factor in explaining why prisons may have an over-representation of adults living with FASD.

- *Will the child have FASD if the pregnant mother drank during any given week?* There is no way to give an absolute answer to this question. As stated above, once the egg has been fertilised, the process of development begins. The advice is that stopping alcohol use at any stage in pregnancy enhances the potential for a healthy outcome in the offspring. The clear message in education is that if you are trying to conceive or planning to become pregnant, it is best to avoid alcohol.

- *Does FASD apply only to certain societies and cultures?* FASD as discussed in this book is caused solely by an alcohol-exposed pregnancy. The physiological nature of pregnancy is not altered or changed by race, culture or religion; therefore, FASD can be a presenting risk factor wherever or whenever alcohol is consumed during pregnancy.

IS FASD A NEW PHENOMENON?

It has been suggested for centuries that alcohol and pregnancy do not mix, but it is only 40 years ago that the term 'fetal alcohol syndrome' was first used in *The Lancet* medical journal. Significant advancements have been made in diagnosis, surveillance, prevention and intervention in some countries (mainly the US and Canada); however, many of these advancements have not been recognised when it comes to coordinated and holistic public health policy responses in the developed world of 2014. Global media outlets have not rushed to print and publicise the vast array of research findings which outline the toxic danger of alcohol to the unborn child and the detrimental array of effects. Ironically, it can be easier to find significant media coverage of 'condoning alcohol use in pregnancy', especially in Europe. This is mainly due to the fact that media outlets tend to focus on those studies which 'condone' use more readily than the vast bodies of academic studies outlining the harm. The Edmonton Charter of September 2013 summarises this concern in the following consensus statement with stark clarity:

> When a million babies are born every year with permanent brain injury from a known and preventable cause, the response ought to be immediate, determined, sustainable and effective.

Historically, the seminal moments of understanding on PAE are as follows:

- The Bible, Judges 13:7, reads: 'Behold thou shalt conceive, and bear a son; and now drink no wine nor strong drink...'

- Greek philosopher Aristotle (384–322 BC) suggested that children of alcoholics were often 'morose and languid'.

- In the eighteenth century, the removal of taxation from alcohol in the UK saw a sharp rise in alcohol consumption, leading many to believe that the rise in prenatal death and birth defects was a direct consequence.

- In 1726 a group of doctors at the Royal College of Physicians of London described children born to alcoholic mothers as 'weak, feeble and distempered'.

- Sullivan (1899) found that women incarcerated in a Liverpool prison gave birth to children with a pattern of birth defects or had higher rates of miscarriage. He noted that women incarcerated for longer periods within the nine months of gestation gave birth to healthier offspring – presumably because imprisonment implies enforced abstinence from alcohol.

- Lemoine *et al.* (1968) discovered in 127 prenatally exposed children distinct features which they referred to as 'alcoholic embryopathy'. It is generally held that the impact of this study was not seen due to the fact that it was written in French. Also the paper published by Lemoine and colleagues did not present any diagnostic tools and therefore did not have the desired impact of promoting recognition of FAS either in France or elsewhere in Europe; however, what it did do was confirm alcohol's teratogenic effects on the fetus or child.

- Findings similar to those of Lemoine *et al.* were found in France, Germany and Sweden.

- Jones and Smith (1973) coined the term 'fetal alcohol syndrome' as an identification of a specific pattern of growth retardation, malformations and CNS defects in children of alcoholic mothers. These eight children had been referred to the Washington Clinic of Ken Jones and David Smith by social workers for 'failure to thrive'. It is here that we get the first direct link to the child welfare system and perhaps the motivation of this book! However, this paper published in *The Lancet* was pivotal as it offered guidance on how to diagnose the disorder of FAS, a component missing in the published work of Lemoine and colleagues in 1968.

- In 1981 the US Surgeon General first advised that pregnant women should not consume any alcohol while pregnant. This was the first government official in the Western world to issue such a warning.

- In 1989, with the trigger statement of the US Surgeon General in 1981, the US progressed to mandatory warning labels on alcoholic drinks explicitly stating the risks to women if they drink while pregnant.

- In 1996 the US Institute of Medicine (IOM) differentiated five separate outcomes of PAE. These outcomes were:

  ○ fetal alcohol syndrome (FAS) with confirmed maternal alcohol exposure

  ○ fetal alcohol syndrome (FAS) without confirmed maternal alcohol exposure

- ◦ partial fetal alcohol syndrome (PFAS) with confirmed maternal alcohol exposure

- ◦ alcohol-related neurodevelopment disorder (ARND)

- ◦ alcohol-related birth defects (ARBD).

- The Centers for Disease Control (2004) affirmed the term 'FASD' within a statewide education process.

- Canadian Diagnostic Guidelines were published. These guidelines were seen as harmonising the approaches to FASD alongside the IMO guidelines of 1996 and the 4-Digit Diagnostic Code of Astley and Clarren (1999), bringing the two approaches of the US and Canada into unison.

- In 2013 the term 'neurobehavioural disorder as a result of prenatal alcohol exposure' (ND-PAE) emerged in DSM-5.

Above is a selection of just some of the key markers of the subject from the first entry in the Bible to, ironically, the 'bible' of psychiatric disorders (DSM-5) published in May 2013. The American Psychiatric Association uses the DSM-5 to classify disorders and has introduced the new term of 'neurobehavioural disorder as a result of prenatal alcohol exposure' (ND-PAE) to identify the conditions related to PAE. Perhaps more significantly, this term has introduced a billable code for physicians. The code found on page 86 of the new manual is 315.8. This is seen by many in the world of FASD research and advocacy as a pivotal entry: if it is billable, it is seeable, and therefore it exists. This may assist physicians in recognising the unseen disability of FASD within their clinics, and helps us move away from the terminology of 'an invisible disability' that has prevailed in the literature to this point. It is a widely held belief that the current term of alcohol-related neurodevelopmental disorder (ARND) is largely unrecognised by society, with this condition often masked behind Asperger syndrome or attention deficit hyperactivity disorder. ARND is considered the most prevalent of all the FASD diagnoses, and evidence is emerging which cites ARND as a disability affecting a large number of children in both foster care and adoption services. It is a most welcome development that the DSM-5 addresses the issue of FASD (albeit with the new term, ND-PAE) and recognises it as a mental health condition.

THE SCIENCE OF ALCOHOL HARM

Before looking at how alcohol impacts the developing fetus, it is worth considering alcohol use in the adult context. Most of us have witnessed or experienced the outward signs of heavy or moderate drinking: the stumbling walk, slurred words, memory lapses and sometimes even aggressive, antisocial behaviour. People who have been drinking have trouble with their balance, judgement and coordination. They react slowly to stimuli, which is why drinking before driving is so dangerous. We see the evidence of a destructive power that alcohol as a toxin has on the developed brain of an adult individual. It can cause the most competent intellectual human being to lose track of their lifestyle, and in the worse cases to lose family, career and home – all for the love of alcohol through a pervasive addiction. All of these physical signs occur because of the way alcohol affects the brain and CNS.

Alcohol has the ability to travel directly to the adult brain and alter its working mechanisms within a short period of time, crucially altering the neurotransmitters. These neurotransmitters function in our brain to carry messages or signals throughout the body and control fundamental human behaviours such as thought processes, behaviour and emotions. The brain is a powerful, unique creation that is unmatched by any human endeavours. It has around 100 billion neurons or nerve cells and around 100 trillion synaptic connections. It is these 'synaptic' connections that are vital to living a healthy and normal life. Unlike a powerful computer, we do not have to write a programme or install a software update in order to get the best outcomes. The brain has the unique ability to programme itself and send instructions throughout the human body to keep it functioning – that is, of course, if the brain is left to its own devices and allowed to naturally produce the chemicals it needs to function normally.

Alcohol also has the ability to increase dopamine, a brain-produced chemical that creates the feeling of pleasure. In this case, the increased dopamine production will fool the drinker into enjoying the activity of drinking. We say 'fool' because for many people the following day is not the best: the head hurts – the brain's way of realigning the natural processes of chemical production, and in this realignment it may send out signals of pain as it struggles to realign its natural balance. Therefore, if the effects are visible in the brain of an adult, it is not a massive leap to consider how it might affect the developing brain of an unborn child.

This reflective piece on alcohol intake in the adult context is used to demonstrate the impact of alcohol on the CNS on a typical basis. This attempts to move the concept of alcohol harm from an abstract and unrecognised context to one which can be readily and easily understood. If alcohol can debilitate an adult, then that serves to underline the potential harm that it can do to an unborn child. Because alcohol can travel freely through the mother's bloodstream to that of her unborn child, once it enters the bloodstream of the fetus through the umbilical cord, it goes to work on the CNS in much the same fashion that we just discussed in the adult context. The adult recovers from the hangover the next day, and it is assumed that the unborn child recovers in the same way. Whilst that may be true to some extent, the difference is in the metabolism rate.

It has been demonstrated in scientific papers that the unborn child metabolises alcohol at a much slower rate than that of the adult mother. The prolongation of the alcohol concentration and the time that exposure might occur could be significant to the developing embryo or fetus (CDC 2004). To understand the effects on the unborn child, it is essential to understand the key areas of how the human body handles absorption, distribution, metabolism and elimination. The sections below are adapted from the CDC Allied Health Education Manual.

Absorption

When a woman drinks alcohol, the absorption/metabolism of the molecule C_2H_5OH occurs rapidly. Peak blood ethanol concentrations are attained approximately one hour after consumption. Women attain consistently greater blood ethanol concentrations than men following equivalent amounts of ethanol. When an alcohol-containing drink is consumed, the alcohol is quickly absorbed in the blood by diffusion and is then transported to the tissues and throughout the water-containing portions of the body as part of the process of distribution. About 20 per cent of the alcohol is absorbed through the stomach, and about 80 per cent is absorbed through the upper portion of the small intestine.

Distribution

Due to alcohol's rapid solubility in water, it can easily cross cell membranes into the cell (which is 98% water). Alcohol is less soluble into lipids and compartments with substantial lipids. The placenta acts as a selective barrier. Alcohol is easily passed by diffusion from the maternal blood into the fetal bloodstream within this mechanism.

Metabolism and elimination

Alcohol is metabolised by enzymes as it is available by concentration. Most ethanol is metabolised in the liver via three pathways:

- alcohol dehydrogenase (ADH)

- microsomal ethanol oxidising system

- catalase (peroxisomal).

Metabolism occurs primarily through the ADH pathway; chronic exposure might enhance or induce other pathways. All metabolism pathways lead to acetaldehyde, which is then metabolised by acetaldehyde dehydrogenase (ALDH); ALDH metabolises acetaldehyde to acetate, which is then metabolised into carbon dioxide and water.

Metabolism refers to the process by which the body breaks down food to extract energy from it. With respect to alcohol, metabolism refers to the transformation of ethanol to acetaldehyde and other products. The primary site of alcohol metabolism is the liver. Only a tiny fraction (less than 10%) of the alcohol consumed is not metabolised and excreted from the body in breath, sweat and urine. (This is why you will never be in a licensed premises that sells alcohol without the service of bathrooms!) This process of metabolism and excretion is known as elimination. The concentration of alcohol in breath and urine mirrors the concentration of alcohol in blood. This means that alcohol in breath can be detected, measured and used to calculate a person's blood alcohol concentration (BAC). The BAC calculation is the standard means of determining the extent of a person's alcohol impairment. A key fact to remember is that humans vary widely in their ability to absorb and eliminate alcohol. This can be a factor in the 'Russian roulette' aspect of alcohol use in pregnancy. Put simply, absorption and elimination rates may be quicker in some people's genetic make-up and may be a protective factor to the unborn child in others.

It must be reiterated that the developing fetus will not have a fully formed liver to metabolise the alcohol in its bloodstream and therefore cannot eliminate the alcohol effectively. It is important to remember that in discussing the science of the impact of alcohol on the developing fetus that other illegal and legal drugs can also present risks in pregnancy. There are many teratogens (substances that can interfere with the normal development of a fetus) including substances of abuse, lead, certain medications and toxins; however, of all the substances of abuse that women might use during pregnancy, alcohol has the most serious, long-lasting effects. It is also the most common teratogen used by women during pregnancy in the Western world.

THINKING OF HAVING A BABY?

Abstaining from alcohol before you become pregnant will increase your chances of having a healthy baby. You will lower your risk of:

- miscarriage or still birth

- having a baby with physical defects

- having a baby with neurodevelopmental deficits such as an intellectual disability.

There is no known safe level of alcohol in pregnancy.

> Every time I hear another media report questioning the not-drinking-in-pregnancy message, my head explodes. If you can stop, do!
>
> (Tammy James [Canada] to child living with FASD)

THE DEVELOPING NERVOUS SYSTEM

Development of the CNS begins around the third week of pregnancy and continues throughout the pregnancy and post-birth. An estimated 95–100 billion neurons are found in the human cortex (Pakkenberg and Gundersen 1997), making the rate of generation nearly 250,000 new neurons formed in the cortex alone each minute of the nine-month gestational period. This period of CNS development is characterised by periods of rapid growth and periods of slower growth as the brain develops. It is thought by some researchers that alcohol has a greater destructive ability in the periods of rapid growth than in periods of slower growth. During this time of neuron development a multitude of events are taking place. The neurons migrate into position to facilitate a lifelong brain function, and synapse formations occur between the neurons and the CNS. Although synapse formations continue throughout life, the developing stage of the CNS pre-birth is marked by a rapid and explosive period in this period of connectivity. This period is also crucially important for the production of the myelin sheath, a process known as myelination, which begins in week 14 of development and continues post-birth through infancy and into adolescence.

Figure 1.1 (page 31) outlines the significant stages of development in utero. Exposure of the developing fetus to alcohol in the *first trimester* is most closely associated with the full effects of FAS, which carries the visible features and serious intellectual damage; however, as can be seen, the fetus is developing essential and critical components of life throughout the nine months of gestation.

What is known and accepted is that the presence of alcohol in the first trimester has the ability to cause significant destruction to cell development with devastating results, the most serious of which is spontaneous abortion. The process of totipotency (the ability of a cell to divide and produce) is significantly prevented by the teratogenic effect of alcohol in the mother's bloodstream. As such, if not causing spontaneous abortion, alcohol has the ability to severely disrupt the natural CNS development and leave the developing brain with missing connections throughout life. It only takes the loss of a small quantity of neurons for the 'patchwork quilt' of the CNS to malfunction with devastating consequences for the individual throughout their lifespan. The level and severity of cell destruction at this stage may impact on how the FASD child navigates the complex world in post-birth development stages. The severe end of neuron loss and destruction may be evidenced in very marked physical presentations in the newborn – that is, FAS.

During the second and third trimesters, the tissues and organs largely have been formed; however, some organs and systems, such as the CNS, remain susceptible to potential damage or alteration caused by the presence of alcohol, reinforcing the message that there is no safe time to consume alcohol during the nine months of pregnancy. The long period of development of the CNS increases its vulnerability to the teratogenic effects of alcohol and other drugs. New insights are helping us to understand more accurately what is happening during the second and third trimesters of CNS development. A study currently underway at Wayne State University and the Perinatology Research Branch of the National Institute of Child Health and Human Development in Detroit is finding very startling results using MRI in the 24–36 weeks of fetal development. Researchers are now able to examine fetal brains and visually track brain communication-network developments in the last trimester of pregnancy with much less invasive methods. They have found that the fetal brain makes essential connections in its development phase pre-birth, contrary to previous belief that the brain begins to make such connections only after birth. The scans also indicate that there is improved maturation in brain connectivity that comes with age. This reiterates critical CNS development in utero throughout all trimesters and highlights how the presence of alcohol can derail this essential development stage. (The study was published in *Science Translational Medicine* in February 2013.)

> There is no safe level of alcohol during all three trimesters of pregnancy. This was news to me! I want to share it with my female friends.
>
> (Niamh C, social worker, Dublin, Ireland, 9 May 2013)

It is important to remember that other areas of development are equally at risk including the eyes and ears, which are intrinsically linked to the developing nervous system. What is also found is the link to teeth once the newborn begins to develop. Where the CNS is impaired and the wiring is out of place, the messages for producing enamel for healthy growth and strong teeth can be absent. This can lead to a very young child presenting with advanced tooth decay. Sadly, the untrained assessor in child welfare interventions (i.e. the social worker) is more likely to assign this symptom to wilful neglect. This is how and where we begin to see FASD children over-represented within our child welfare systems. The difficulty for child welfare professionals in identifying this neurobehavioural profile in child welfare and neglect cases can only be addressed by skill-based education and training within their work settings.

> She had 14 cavities. We had dental surgery to put on seven crowns and pull one out. The other six either fell out or were about to fall out by the time we did the surgery. Her adenoids completely covered her nasal passage, so these were removed and tubes were put in her ears to drain the fluid that had built up there. Then we fixed her crossed eyes: two muscles in one eye and one in the other. We also patched her good eye for one and a half years in total.
>
> (Anonymous adoptive mother, Canada)

Exposure to alcohol during all periods of development might result in major structural or functional abnormalities. The minority of around 0.02–0.05 per 1000 births of those affected in the womb will have the structural, visible features. It's the remainder, estimated at 9–10 per 1000 births, that will suffer with the invisible brain injury but maintain a normal physical development. These statistics are generally accepted as a benchmark by which to address FASD within different cultures. As you will notice in this book, prevalence rates can vary greatly, as for the most part they are only estimates.

Individuals might have cognitive and/or behavioural impairments, problems with language, memory issues, difficulty with visual–spatial learning, attention disorders, reduced reaction times, dysmaturity and deficits in functioning, such as planning and organising. These impairments may occur in all individuals with FASD, on a range of mild to severe. As they progress in life, their impairments from the CNS harm can become more pronounced as society begins to demand more by way of adhering to the expected 'norms' of rules and regulations. The impact is lifelong. It is the range of outcomes as a result of PAE that encompasses all categories under the FASD term. These factors are considered in more detail in Chapter 3.

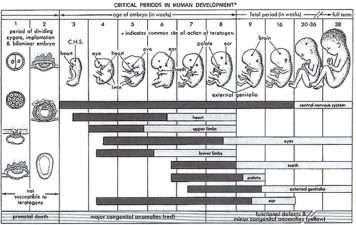

Figure 1.1 The significant stages of development in utero
(adapted from Moore, Persaud and Torchia, 2011)

FASD AND POST-BIRTH EXPERIENCE

With the additional mix of poverty, parental mental illness and domestic violence, the snowball effect within the family unit can be catastrophic and one that may only be helped by the considerable outside support of qualified and skilled professionals. If a child with a fetal alcohol injury resulting in sensory-integration difficulties is living in poverty, their ability to manage and regulate their behaviours could be severely compromised such that they may encounter unpleasant antisensory stimuli (e.g. dirt, smells, incessant noises, chaotic comings and goings). Their unregulated behaviour stemming from the sensory-integration difficulties are more likely to be viewed by the social services agent as being in a category of neglect and poor attachment, resulting in the child being removed from the family and placed in the state care system or residential or foster care. If intervention professionals had an understanding of sensory difficulties stemming from fetal brain injury due to alcohol, the potential to redirect service provision and try differently with the child and family might prevent family breakdown and removal of the child. (We return to this area of practice in Chapter 3 with tips and strategies to identify and work with sensory dysfunction.)

It is important to consider that healthy diet, exercise and a healthy living environment can reduce prevalence rates; however, it is also important to note that alcohol consumption in pregnancy can and does cancel out the benefits of healthy life choices. Hutson *et al.* (2012) demonstrated in a study that folic acid transport to the developing fetus is compromised in pregnancy by heavy and chronic alcohol use. The study remarked that decreased levels of folic acid to the developing fetus may be a contributing factor to the deficits found within FASD. The study strongly recommended that health professionals continue to counsel pregnant women and women of child-bearing age on the proper folic acid supplements as well as giving the clear message that abstinence from alcohol is the only safe approach for a healthy pregnancy. This study focused only on the heavy use of alcohol in pregnancy, and the study identified the need for low-level and moderate use to be studied in relation to folic acid benefits when any alcohol is consumed.

Because any individual with an FASD is the product of a unique interaction of dose and timing of alcohol exposure as well as experiences, the service needs of affected individuals and their families can differ significantly; however, some general areas of service and specific services have been identified that are universally beneficial, including a nurturing and structured caregiving environment, parent and service provider education about FASD, and a thorough multidisciplinary evaluation to identify individual strengths and weaknesses (Streissguth 1997). Families and caregivers are essential in the treatment planning process (Chasnoff 2011).

The diverse nature of persons living with FASD makes an interdisciplinary team approach extremely important and essential. A diagnostic physician requires a significant amount of case history of the individual when considering a diagnosis for a neurobehavioural condition associated with PAE. The collective contribution of professionals and caregivers is crucial to a successful diagnosis and the post-diagnosis support/care plan. If a child does not get a holistic and focused intervention along with their diagnosis, the prognosis may be limited. Giving the estimated high prevalence rates within our societies and communities, and the lifelong effects of FASD, the social suffering and economic cost burden is significant to all.

BEHAVIOURS RESULTING FROM FAULTY BRAIN WIRING

When children with FASD fail to comply with the norms, rules and regulations of society, this non-compliance may be attributed to faulty wiring in the brain rather than being viewed in the context of a bad child who is wilful in their non-compliance with basic requests. When a child knows how to recite their ten times tables one day but completely forgets the next, this can be due to brain injury – in this case short-term memory. The child may exhibit problems in storing and processing the information for later use, as the brain wiring is just not feeding the correct storage unit in the brain. In the words of Professor Barry Carpenter OBE who holds the iNet Chair in Special Education, with the FASD child 'it is here today but gone tomorrow'. Professor Carpenter has described FASD in the British education system as a ticking 'time bomb' due to society's lack of awareness of the disability.

In many Western societies we are seeing an explosion of neurobehavioural diagnoses being applied quickly to the child that does not conform to the norm of expectations and stages of development. ('At ten years old you should be able to perform these tasks. This is what ten-year-olds do!') For the most part, the international body of evidence demonstrates that children with FASD do not typically do as well as they progress into their teens and young adulthood. They can struggle to lead independent lives and may develop severe and complex secondary disabilities. According to research by Streissguth *et al.* (1996), an estimated 90 per cent may develop mental illness, around 60 per cent will find themselves in trouble with the law and incarcerated, and around 40 per cent will develop destructive drug and alcohol behaviours. In other words, if society fails to recognise the primary disability of FASD, the significant psychosocial challenges of homelessness, addiction, mental illness and criminality may emerge. The cost burden to society is staggering at a time when global health budgets are being squeezed. Skilled and trained foster carers, adoptive parents and professionals can have a dramatic impact on ameliorating a child's development of secondary disabilities. The provision of a stable and secure home life can mitigate some of the challenges faced by this cohort of children, and those adopted or fostered into safe, structured caregiving environments may have a better outcome. The majority of children living with FASD have been through foster care for some part – if not all – of their childhood. In this context foster parents play a significant role in mitigating the development of secondary disabilities, and for this they need to be acknowledged, supported and valued in their role of FASD prevention; however, it is important that foster care providers promote caregiver stress-reduction initiatives through increased access to flexible respite care services. Simply put, caring for a child with a neurodevelopmental or neurobehavioural condition is a 24/7 task. Foster carers need the understanding and support of the social service provision in maintaining the placement and preventing disruption.

FASD AND DEVELOPMENTAL DELAY

The term 'developmental delay' abounds when a child begins to demonstrate a failure to achieve that which is laid down as the 'norm' described above. Children develop at their own pace, and the typical range may be quite wide for some. It is important to note that there can be a multiplicity of reasons for a child not achieving the expected norms of development. They may suffer from genetic weakness resulting in an intellectual disability not linked to an alcohol-exposed pregnancy, or suffer through adverse living conditions in the first five years or may have developed structural brain abnormalities due to what is now known as 'toxic stress' (Harvard Briefing Paper 1 see http://developingchild.harvard.edu/resources/briefs).

Children with FASD often perform much lower developmentally than their chronological age resulting in their not being able to effectively engage or interact within their own peer settings. They may demonstrate a lack of social competence, poor impulse control and an inability to concentrate. Such behaviours start to spell long-term risks such as failing or dropping out of education as well as implications for employment opportunities later. Sadly for this cohort of children, many of the interventions offered in response to such behaviours are the *wrong* interventions. The helping professions reaching out to these young people may mistakenly use interventions that support a fundamental belief that the brain is intact, and that it is just the environmental impact of neglect, poor parenting, parental mental illness, domestic violence or parental addiction to drugs and alcohol that has knocked this young person off their normal trajectory in life. There may be a faulty expectation that traditional interventions, such as behaviour-modification techniques, psychotherapy or counselling, will return this young person to normal functioning; however, this will not work for the person with FASD. Their brain is 'miswired' or damaged, and this wiring cannot be rectified through such interventions. What works one day may not work the next. Traditional interventions are likely to fail without the interventionist questioning *why* they have failed. This is fundamentally where we are losing these children to the long-term risks outlined above. If we fail to understand them, then they will fail to understand *us* and choose a path that fits their brain function. If, on the other hand, practitioners are fully aware of these children's needs, then their brain function can be accommodated by simple but effective tweaks of our environment, language, expectations and interventions. They need caring interventions that are tailored to an organic brain injury. Traditional methods, theories and beliefs will only compound the difficulties for these children and their caregivers.

CROSSOVER NEUROBEHAVIOURAL CONDITIONS

Current evidence would contend that we are not seeing this neurobehavioural disability in the context of an alcohol-exposed pregnancy; instead, the characteristics in a child may be viewed as suffering from attention deficit disorder, oppositional defiance disorder, autism spectrum disorder or the most common in our child care services, attention deficit hyperactivity disorder. A child may be put on serious pharmacological agents to treat behaviours without thought being given to what lies behind the behaviour – treating the symptom without considering a cause. This is similar to saying that in treating cancer in smokers we should not consider nicotine as a causal agent. Where we do assign a causal agent to a child's dysfunctional behaviour, it tends to be generalisations and traditional thinking related to the environment or poor parenting, without any real depth or analysis given to the possible causal agent(s). Where alcohol is a present feature in parenting, the consideration of FASD should not be ignored when dealing with developmental delay and behavioural symptoms. FASD needs to be on the checklist of considerations.

SUPPORTING RESEARCH EVIDENCE

An FASD diagnostic process will seek to analyse the specific behaviours that are presenting by listening to the concerns of parent, carer or teacher. Alongside this, a diagnosis will seek a full developmental history of the child and also perform complete psychological and neuropsychological testing as part of a holistic assessment process. Here again we see the importance of the multidisciplinary role in assessment of FASD. Many professionals and carers hold vital and valuable information of a chronology of time that will be vital to a successful diagnosis of FASD. Below we look again at some of the core domains that may be affected by an alcohol-exposed pregnancy and how this may be represented in daily living of the individual. Although the facial dysmorphology and growth deficits associated with PAE are perhaps more easily identified, the most damaging effects are abnormalities of the CNS, which affect neurocognitive functioning. A growing body of research has shown that individuals exposed to alcohol prenatally exhibit 'structural alterations…in brain size, shape, and symmetry' (McGee and Riley 2006, p.46). Additionally, abnormalities in specific brain structures, including the corpus callosum, cerebellum and basal ganglia, are well documented (McGee and Riley 2006; Riley and McGee 2005; Riley, McGee and Sowell 2004; Spadoni *et al.* 2007).

In general, the majority of alcohol-exposed individuals do not have significant intellectual disabilities, but individuals with FASD exhibit lower overall intellectual functioning compared with the general population (Mattson *et al.* 1997; May *et al.* 2006; Streissguth and O'Malley 2000). For example, a sample of 415 adolescent and adult patients diagnosed with FAS had a mean IQ of 80, and those diagnosed with fetal alcohol effects (FAE) had a mean IQ of 88 (Streissguth *et al.* 2004). In a sample of children with PAE, Mattson *et al.* (1997) found a mean IQ of 74 among those who met full criteria for FAS, and a mean IQ of 83 for those who did not exhibit the physical features of FAS.

Additionally, evidence for some consistent neurocognitive deficits has emerged and appears to be prominent in individuals with PAE: verbal learning and memory problems; attention deficits; problems in abstract and practical reasoning; and problems in executive functioning characterised by difficulties in planning, organising and sequencing behaviour (Adams *et al.* 2001; Coles 1997; Connor *et al.* 2000; Kodituwakku 2007; Kodituwakku *et al.* 2001; Mattson and Riley 1998; Mattson *et al.* 1999; Rasmussen 2005).

Executive-functioning deficits in the areas of complex nonverbal problem solving (Mattson *et al.* 1999), flexible thinking (Kodituwakku *et al.* 1995; Mattson *et al.* 1999; Olson *et al.* 1998; Schonfeld *et al.* 2001) and behavioural inhibition (Kodituwakku *et al.* 1995; Mattson *et al.* 1999) have also been reported. Importantly, these deficits are found both in exposed individuals who meet the full criteria for FAS and those who do not (Connor *et al.* 2000; Kodituwakku *et al.* 2001; Mattson *et al.* 1998, 1999), and they persist into adulthood (Connor *et al.* 2000; Olson *et al.* 1998; Streissguth and O'Malley 2000; Streissguth *et al.* 1991).

Moreover, executive functioning problems do not appear to be merely a reflection of lower cognitive abilities among individuals with PAE, that is, deficits in executive functioning have been found to be greater in exposed individuals than would be expected based on IQ scores (Connor *et al.* 2000), and other studies have demonstrated that problems with executive functioning are still apparent when controlling for IQ (Kodituwakku *et al.* 2001; Schonfeld *et al.* 2001). A number of researchers have also examined the association between PAE and adaptive functioning, or the ability to independently perform developmentally expected tasks associated with daily living, such as self-care as well as communication and social skills.

Chapter 2

FASD RECOGNITION, SCREENING AND DIAGNOSIS

RECOGNITION OF FASD

Initial recognition that a child or older individual has a potential problem can come from many sources. Often, parents notice differences between a child and his or her siblings. Recognition of many of the problems associated with FASD are the sorts of things that visits to the doctor's office are meant to identify. It is assumed that triggers, such as facial abnormalities, growth delay, developmental problems or maternal alcohol use, will emerge from the contact. Recognition of a potential problem should lead the provider, regardless of specific profession, to facilitate getting the child and his or her family to the appropriate next step such as a developmental paediatrician.

School systems and day-care staff interact with a large number of children and often recognise when someone is having difficulty. The spectrum of brain differences with FASD varies among individuals and may cause different learning, behavioural and daily living challenges for the child or adult with whom you are working or for whom you are caring. Social service professionals, clinical staff, early-years workers, social workers and foster care agencies frequently recognise children and individuals experiencing challenges and difficulties who may be in need of an evaluation. Finally, health care providers (particularly paediatricians) are often the first to detect problems; or obstetricians, who might be aware of a maternal substance-misuse issue and might refer a newborn. In many situations, especially in the foster and adoptive populations, it may not be known if the child was born from an alcohol-exposed pregnancy. This should not deter them from seeking an evaluation with a diagnostic service. It is as relevant to rule out an FASD condition as it is to confirm one.

An individual should be referred for screening or diagnosis when there is any report of concern by a parent or caregiver (foster or adoptive parent) that his or her child is displaying neurocognitive behaviours that do not have a clear cause and if there are facial, growth or CNS abnormalities present in the child. In making a referral for a complete diagnostic evaluation for FAS, it is helpful for the referring provider to gather and document specific data related to the FAS criteria. These data will assist the provider in making the decision to diagnose the child or to refer the child to a multidisciplinary evaluation team to evaluate and guide the diagnostic process. A complete review of systems, noting features consistent with FAS, will be most productive.

When considering taking that initial step of seeking a diagnosis, our minds may naturally flow to a physician sitting in a medical environment. This is true for so many of the conditions but is not necessarily the case when discussing or seeking a diagnosis of FASD. It is key to remember that any diagnosis for FASD is best done by a collective and collaborative act of all professionals in a child's life. Pre-diagnostic information gathered by a social worker or caregiver is an essential and imperative component to a successful assessment. A good standard to be set in diagnostic environments is to have a team assessment and arrive at a mutually accepted diagnosis with care-planning recommendations.

If this is done collaboratively, it naturally derives benefits of supports and appropriate interventions to the child and family from the knowledge within the team for the post-diagnosis life. Once a diagnosis is received, it is important to remember that the diagnosed condition is for life and the child is likely to need individually tailored supports, guidance and interventions into and during adulthood. Child welfare practitioners need to be well informed of the needs of such clients living with FASD and provide holistic and skilled interventions to support the caring task by parents. A care plan rooted in the knowledge of FASD-focused interventions is imperative.

Key points

- A diagnosis does not change the child/adult. What it does is help those caring for the individual to understand the way they are learning and developing and the neurobehavioural challenges that the individual is experiencing. A diagnosis can help everyone understand the child/adult at their developmental stage rather than at their chronological age.

- The most effective interventions for individuals living with FASD is when those around them understand the cognitive dysfunction that they are carrying. If the individual is being judged as non-compliant by society due to a lack of understanding of their condition, this can have far-reaching implications for behaviour and compliance with the expected norms. Children with CNS difficulties are more likely to 'drop' out of formal education due to their non-competency status. It is believed that this is one of the key factors of individuals sliding into secondary disabilities of mental health, homelessness and criminal justice issues. A key for post-diagnostic life is to have skilled and trained allied health and social care professionals who understand the complexities of living with FASD post-diagnosis.

- In some communities, diagnostic services may be difficult to access due to the public policy on FASD in those communities, or indeed just from being rural, isolated communities; however, it should be possible to access some level of services depending on your public policy, if not in state-funded services then perhaps in private or voluntary capacity. A case example of this would be Ireland. Although cited at an 80 per cent drinking rate in pregnancy (McCarthy *et al.* 2013), it has no statewide diagnostic facility or national diagnostic guidelines. It does, however, have a 2.5-day private diagnostic service in Dublin.

- A diagnosis will not 'magic away' the concerns that were present prior to seeking an assessment. What it offers is a starting point to seek a care plan that provides the correct intervention, one that moves from traditional responses of care planning to one that recognises the disability and provides interventions to match the need. Again we return to a key need in this regard. A care plan in any context is delivered by a collection of different professionals, delivering a holistic package of care for both client and family.

Joseph had 15 different professionals and school support before we finally got a diagnosis.

(Anonymous adoptive mother, Canada)

SCREENING TOOLS

What can be beneficial to a parent, carer or professional is to access screening tools which can identify whether FASD is a possible cause affecting the presenting behaviour of an individual. A key issue that still prevails within the world of FASD diagnosis is when to screen for a neurobehavioural diagnosis that has an absence of any facial or physical features. It is evident that the condition most associated with neurobehavioural dysfunction is alcohol-related neurodevelopmental disorder (ARND). A difficulty with this 'invisible' disorder is that it will slowly manifest as the child grows. For many adoptive, foster and indeed birth parents this manifestation of the condition does not appear until we begin to ask the child to conform to the norms of expected development, a time when the child begins to draw on those parts of the brain to understand the world of rules and regulations by which we are governed. Within child development, the age of five or six years is when the child is expected to have in their command around 2000 words and understand the basic rules of responsibility and accomplishment. From here we begin to expect the child to conform to school rules, develop strategies to cope with transitions as they progress through the school years and learn the normal codes of what is expected of good and bad behaviours. In assessing for neurobehavioural dysfunction it is thought to be best by many researchers to wait until a child is in full flow of cognitive functions where they are old enough to comply with family and societal requirements. So in some instances FASD may not appear until the child is much older or is in high school.

When considering the option of screening, professionals can access a very comprehensive and approved tool in the Neurobehavioral Screening Test (NST) developed in Canada by Dr Gideon Koren and colleagues (Koren, Zelner and Nash 2014) at the Motherisk Program in the Toronto Children's Hospital. The NST is validated for children between the ages of 6 and 13 years and can greatly help in identifying the signs of FASD as they present at this developmental stage. It should be used by health or social work by interviewing the primary caregiver of the child. Again, it is of critical importance that the NST be seen purely as a *screening* tool – it is not a diagnostic tool.

SCREENING CHECKLIST FOR THE FASD BEHAVIOURAL PHENOTYPE

Step 1: Identifying behaviour suggestive of FASD

The following questions should be asked of the child's parent/guardian to determine whether the child's behaviour is suggestive of FASD:

1. Does your child act too young for his/her age?
2. Does your child have difficulty concentrating, and cannot pay attention for long?
3. Is your child disobedient at home?
4. Does your child lie or cheat?
5. Does your child lack guilt after misbehaving?
6. Does your child act impulsively and without thinking?
7. Does your child have difficulty sitting still/is restless/hyperactive?

(If the parent/caregiver answers yes to at least six out of seven items, this is suggestive of FASD with 86% sensitivity and 82% specificity.)

If the child does not exhibit behaviour consistent with attention deficit hyperactivity disorder (ADHD) (i.e. answer is negative for questions 2, 6, 7), then a score of three out of the four following questions needs to be positive:

1. Does your child lack guilt after misbehaving?
2. Does your child lie or cheat?
3. Is your child disobedient at home?
4. Does your child act too young for his/her age?

Step 2: Differentiating FASD from ADHD

The child needs to exhibit two of the following three characteristics:

- lack of guilt after misbehaving
- displays acts of cruelty, bullying or meanness to others
- acts young for his/her age; or the child needs to exhibit three of the following six characteristics:
  - lack of guilt after misbehaving
  - displays acts of cruelty, bullying or meanness to others
  - acts young for his/her age
  - steals from home
  - steals outside the home of the home
  - lies and cheats.

From Koren, Zelner and Nash (2014)

Case study 1

A seven-year-old boy with severe learning and behavioural issues is presented. He behaves like a four-year-old boy. His mother says he commonly does not listen to her. He was caught several times telling people he lost money his mother gave him, although he used it to buy sweets. After hitting his younger sibling, he never expresses remorse. He cannot concentrate on a task for more than seven minutes. He is very impulsive and explodes easily. He is all over the place non-stop. He often tortures his cat. He takes money from his mother's purse without her knowing. He took a friend's toy when he visited him.

Scoring: This child achieves the maximum seven positive scores and is screened positive for FASD.

Case study 2

A nine-year-old girl who reads at grade-1 level and cannot do any mathematics is presented. She prefers to play with grade-1 kids. She often does not follow her mother's instructions. No previous cases of lying or cheating have been recorded. She was not remorseful when her little brother fell after she pushed him. She savagely hit a toddler. Her mother stated that several times she took and hid in her bag things belonging to other kids, and she does the same at home.

Scoring: In step 1 this child endorsed only five positive answers. Because she does not present with typical ADHD, you would continue to step 2. Here she endorses three positive scores, which is a positive screen for FASD.

GENETIC SCREENING

A comprehensive medical evaluation will help distinguish between conditions which may present in a similar way. Genetic screening is an early port of call to establish whether there is a genetic component of the neurobehavioural – and at times physical – anomalies present in the child. In some regions, developmental/diagnostic clinics offer this sort of comprehensive assessment in a one-stop shop; however, in many parts of the world, such comprehensive services are not available and the parent, carer or professional will have to source pre-diagnostic assessment services independently. It is in this context that a visit to a geneticist is highly recommended. As stated above, a number of conditions/disabilities have a similar presentation profile and could include the following:

- fetal anticonvulsant embryopathy

- maternal phenylketonuria embryopathy

- Brachmann de Lange or Cornelia de Lange syndrome

- Dubowitz syndrome

- Aarskog syndrome

- Noonan syndrome

- Williams syndrome

- Toluene embryopathy

- Velocardiofacial syndrome

- Kabuki syndrome

- Ritscher-Schinzel syndrome

- chromosomal disorders (several).

Identifying a genetic origin or source for the difficulties the child is experiencing may help the carer or professional better understand the interventions and treatments needed. Whilst parents, carers or professionals are there to promote the well-being of the child, a request for a genetic test may have negative implications for children, and the carer and the health care provider must be prepared to acknowledge and discuss such issues with both the child and the birth family. Currently, a referral in the UK to the public diagnostic facility requires that the child have a genetic screening prior to presentation in the FASD diagnostic services. It therefore follows that the elimination of genetic disorders as a source of the presenting concern will eventually aid and support an FASD diagnostic physician. A positive screen for a genetic condition in the child will obviously present new challenges to the parent, carer or professional; however, a positive identification of a genetic condition will more likely be better understood and received by disability service providers.

Age for screening and diagnosis

Evidence suggests that the optimum age for diagnosis is before the age of six years (Streissguth *et al.* 1996). Sadly, current trends within many countries are slow at acknowledging this lifelong disabling condition within their public health systems, unlike public health responses in the US and Canada. Many developed cultures tend to wait until the child demonstrates failure before seeing the disability. This 'failure' tends to emerge when the child begins to fail in responding to the rules and regulations that society expects him or her to follow. The most obvious conflict area where the child will begin to demonstrate failure is within the education system. Seeing the disability within the first five or six years of life could significantly improve the outcome for the child as they develop. Perhaps with their disability acknowledged, an education route that accepts and understands the needs of the child can be found, thus avoiding an educational breakdown in later years.

VINELAND ADAPTIVE BEHAVIOR SCALE

The second potential for a pre-FASD diagnosis is to undergo an assessment which looks at adaptive functioning. According to the fourth edition of the *Diagnostic and Statistical Manual of Mental Disorders*, adaptive functioning refers to the following:

> How effectively individuals cope with common life demands on how well they meet the standards of personal independence expected of someone in their particular age group, sociocultural background, and community setting. Adaptive functioning may be influenced by various factors, including education, motivation, personality traits, social and vocational opportunities, and the mental disorders and general medical conditions that may coexist with mental retardation.
>
> (American Psychiatric Association 1994, p.40)

The language in this 1994 excerpt is strangely heavy, but for many parents, carers or professionals the sentiments expressed in this description of adaptive function will be something that they can readily identify from their own observations of the child in their care. The Vineland Adaptive Behavior Scale (VABS) is one of the assessment tools which is commonly used for people with FASD. The VABS has been used since the 1930s but perhaps only became more widely used from the mid 1970s in the US. Put simply, a Vineland assessment measures an individual's adaptive functioning across a number of key domains.

The VABS is widely available and can be carried out by a range of professionals. In the US, clinical social workers can and do perform VABS assessments. In the UK and Ireland, educational psychologists would be very skilled in undertaking an assessment. The main point to consider in seeking a VABS is that it is not an assessment specific to any particular disability; instead, it is a standalone assessment tool that crosses *many* neurodevelopmental disabilities. The key ingredient in this assessment is that the individuals must know extensively the person being assessed.

Table 2.1 provides a VABS assessment carried out on a 13-year-old girl who was adopted at six months of age from an Eastern European orphanage by British adopters.

Table 2.1 *Vineland Adaptive Behavior Scale assessment of a 13-year-old girl who had been adopted at the age of six months*

Domain	Functional age (years)/observational data
Daily living skills	
• Domestic tasks	4.7
• Personal skills	5.2
• Community functioning	5.9
Communication	
• Receptive	2.5
• Expressive	7.6
• Written	11.9
Non-verbal communication	No descriptive gestures Inappropriate facial expressions Overly familiar with people
Social play/imagination	
• Coping skills	3.4
• Play and leisure	3.5[a]
• Interpersonal relationships	4.8[b]

a) Much younger play; enveloped in her own interests; no real imagination

b) No preference for carers (i.e. will go to anyone who meets her needs); not able to consider the needs of others

The authors of this book are clear in saying that seeking a Vineland assessment prior to diagnosis is not to underestimate or eradicate the need for a diagnosis. It will, however, offer valuable information if completed prior to an FASD assessment. First, it offers the primary carers a hands-on tool to guide intervention strategies. If you know your 13-year-old child only has a domestic task age of 4.7 years, then your intervention of seeking house chores will be tailored to the age ability – saving many arguments and behavioural meltdowns around house chores! Second, providing such a valuable adaptive behaviour analysis to the FASD diagnostic physician will aid their understanding of the workings of the individual's CNS in their assessment.

ESTABLISHING MATERNAL ALCOHOL USE

It is important to note at this juncture that no matter how much science tells us, even the best studies using the most ethical methodologies and data collection methods can still find it impossible to return definitive results about alcohol use. This is mainly due to the simple fact that the human body and the act of reproduction is a unique and complex act of human nature. Key to a diagnosis of FASD is having the confirmation that alcohol was consumed when the individual was in utero. This is the case for all possible diagnoses except for an allowance made for FAS where the physical evidence is considered to be enough in reaching a diagnostic conclusion.

Identifying prenatal exposure to alcohol is important for an early diagnosis, but information about maternal alcohol consumption is often difficult to obtain. Many children in the foster care and adoption systems simply do not have comprehensive medical records, let alone records of their birth and pre-birth life. This fact is one that confronts many carers today in trying to seek a diagnosis, when evidence of cognitive dysfunction presents itself in daily caring and education environments. A second issue is the frustration that caregivers can often feel when trying to help or intervene, because the individual living with a deficit(s) in executive function may not consider themselves as having a disability. Indeed, it is self-reported by adolescents living with cognitive deficits that they 'would rather be seen as bad than be seen as stupid'.

It has been suggested that measuring the presence of fatty acid ethyl esters (FAEE) in meconium may be used as a 'biomarker' to establish maternal alcohol use and exposure to the unborn. Meconium in layman's terms is the first 'poo' of a newborn. There is strong potential for meconium testing in maternity hospitals to become more universal, but to do so would seek investment in both laboratory systems and allied health education regarding the testing requirements. This would be costly to establish. Currently, the collection of meconium is challenging. The material or waste discharged by the newborn must be collected within a brief time frame following birth, and it must be kept in cold storage and analysed swiftly by trained personnel. Results currently would suggest that not all hospital laboratories have been able to demonstrate consistent results, but under optimum conditions the collection of FAEE in the newborn's first discharges following birth have been demonstrated to be a reliable marker for identifying alcohol and drug use in pregnancy.

There are complex ethical issues around testing for fetal alcohol exposure soon after birth because the question of fetal rights versus maternal rights enter centre stage. Should such a test be carried out only with the express consent of the mother? If a mother refuses such a test, does the child go without a crucial 'biomarker' that may be vitally important to their health needs down the line? These complex questions are beyond the scope of this book. It is for the reader to consider that such mechanisms are now available and to navigate the ethical dilemmas on a case-by-case basis.

THE VALUE OF A DIAGNOSIS

Whilst a diagnosis is for recognition and opening doors to services, welfare benefits, special schooling and job programmes, it is equally important to remember that there are many countries that do not formally recognise FASD within its disability services. In these cultures and communities, the challenges in supporting a newly diagnosed child or adult are immense, as the life lived with an unrecognised disability is likely to encounter lifelong problems and service deficits. Getting as many professionals on-board at the screening stage can reap benefits when and if the child receives a formal diagnosis. Family physicians or general practitioners (GP) need to be fully engaged and supportive of referral to diagnostic facility. Post-diagnosis, the physician/GP can be instrumental in connecting valuable service interventions, while also supporting the parent/caregiver needs with the diagnosis.

It is sometimes suggested to FASD educators that seeking a diagnosis has no positive effect and may have the opposite effect in 'labelling' the child and hindering their development. This view tends to be more prevalent within communities where FASD is not officially recognised by public policy in health and social services; however, it is the view of the authors that to deny an individual – be it a child or an adult – an opportunity for receiving a diagnosis would be a destructive decision both for the child/adult and for society as a whole. Such a decision would only increase the likelihood of major secondary disabilities in later life.

The following account from an adoptive parent demonstrates such needs. In this case both adopted sons were given a diagnosis with FASD in their teens.

> Liam has done phenomenally well and is working hard to become a personal fitness trainer…a lot for him to take on board and deal with, including waking up to acknowledge he has a learning disability and how this hampers his progress and will *always* be a disadvantage in whatever he tackles. But he seems accepting of it all. He also plans to return to school in order to get his school leaving certificate and then progress from there. He turns 18 tomorrow…where did the time fly, and that tiny four-year-old kid we adopted all those years ago! Tom, meanwhile, is 11 months clean today but his mental health status continues to be very fragile and we seem to be making little progress there. I continue to only be able to deal with being around him in small doses because he winds me up so much. It is like a pressure cooker that has been on the boil for 42 days, or like watching a can of beer explode in front of you as soon as he walks in the door!

> (Adoptive mother, Canada)

What many people will experience when concerned that a child is presenting an FASD behavioural phenotype is the lack of a trained diagnostic clinician and multidisciplinary team within their community. Alongside this will be the challenge of assessing the particular behaviour and getting clarity that it is derived from PAE many years earlier. This is why the recording of alcohol use in pregnancy is so vital on the child's file in anti-natal assessment by attending midwives, obstetricians and gynaecology personnel. As mentioned, behaviours stemming from an unseen brain-based cause can have other origins/causes, and this is why we should not pre-judge before a full assessment with a fully qualified multidisciplinary team.

As acknowledged, many communities around the developed world still do not have diagnostic clinics or templates. In such situations it is advisable to harness services that exist within the community for more recognised developmental disabilities; for example, currently many educational programmes contain professionals capable of carrying out neurocognitive assessments such as VABS. In seeking the formal diagnosis, the following is a general guide to the process acknowledging the large disparity that exists within the global context of diagnostic practices. The FASD diagnosis will involve four key areas, which are:

- dysmorphology assessment

- neurobehavioural assessment

- physical examination

- confirmation of PAE while in utero.

The last point is essential to a diagnosis, which is why it is so important that PAE be noted on the medical records at the time of birth. Many diagnostic physicians may refuse to carry out an assessment for FASD if PAE cannot be confirmed. This can prove to be very difficult in the case of adopted children where their biological medical records are incomplete. The confirmation of illicit drug use is often present, but notes on alcohol use may be absent. This again comes back to training for both the adoption agency facilitating the adoption at source and the adoption agency providing continuing services for the adoptive parents.

INTRODUCTION OF A NEW TERM

The term fetal alcohol effects (FAE) was previously used to describe intellectual disabilities and problems with behaviour and learning in a person with PAE but who did not meet the criteria for FAS. In 1996 the Institute of Medicine (IOM) replaced FAE with the terms alcohol-related neurodevelopmental disorder (ARND) and alcohol-related birth defects (ARBD). The new term entering into the field is 'neurodevelopmental disorder as a result of prenatal alcohol exposure' (ND-PAE), which is the description and code designated by DSM-5 to identify PAE which does not fit the FAS criteria.

DIAGNOSTIC TOOLS

Diagnosing under the FASD spectrum is difficult and complex. Diagnosis over the years has varied widely from clinic to clinic and country to country, due to the complex nature of the presenting disability. Typically, a multidisciplinary team thoroughly assesses the child using diagnostic procedures to evaluate dysmorphic (abnormality of shape or form) and growth parameters and to obtain appropriate neurodevelopmental evaluation data. Once a diagnosis is made, an intervention plan is developed by the multidisciplinary team, including dysmorphologists, developmental paediatricians, psychiatrists, psychologists, social workers and educational specialists. Other clinicians, such as paediatricians and family practitioners, might also be involved.

The seminal work by Stratton, Howe and Battaglia (1996) published by the IOM, exploring a diagnostic framework for the four main conditions under the FASD spectrum of conditions, is seen by many to be the foundational publication from which updated guidelines have been derived. Advanced medical technology, such as MRI, promotes the understanding of PAE deficits. The four main diagnostic tools that are in operation today are as follows:

- 4-Digit Diagnostic Code (Astley and Clarren 1999)

- FAS Guidelines (CDC) (Bertrand *et al.* 2004)

- Hoyme FASD Guidelines (2005) (Hoyme *et al.* 2005)

- Fetal Alcohol Spectrum Disorder: Canadian Guidelines for Diagnosis (2005) (Chudley *et al.* 2005).

DIAGNOSTIC CLASSIFICATIONS

The characteristics of FASD fall under three broad domains of human development: growth deficiency, facial dysmorphology and CNS impairment. One of the difficulties in diagnosing within the FASD range is the degree to which any of the above may be present from a mild presentation of symptoms to a more severe presentation. At one end of the spectrum we have full presentation across all three domains, which is FAS. At the other end of the spectrum the individual will usually meet typical requirements for growth and facial features but may have hidden neurocognitive dysfunction and impairment that is causing considerable disruption in meeting the requirements of daily living, schooling or working life. This end of the spectrum is referred to as alcohol-related neurodevelopment disorder (ARND). Some people describe the ARND end of the spectrum as mild, with the FAS as the severe manifestation of alcohol-exposed birth; others completely reverse this analogy, seeing the ARND disability as having more destructive properties in a society that does not recognise or understand the condition. Evidence suggests that if appropriate diagnosis, services and skilled interventions are not in place within our disability/health services, then the prognosis for these children as they develop into adulthood is poor (Streissguth *et al.* 1996). Parents, carers and professionals working with this invisible disability can be faced with many challenges in trying to seek services and support the child in their care.

This was best described to the authors in 2011 during a clinical programme of FASD education when an adoptive mother made the following statement:

> I have two adopted children; one has FAS with all visible signs, the other has ARND with no physical/visible signs. I wish that my ARND son had the visible characteristics of FAS, because at least then society would *see* his disability and accommodate him better and understand his needs.

ARND

When diagnosing within the FASD spectrum, a diagnosis for ARND will need to have supporting evidence of PAE and CNS impairments consistent with alcohol exposure which are not attributable to other genetic, organic or environmental conditions. (Further guidance is given in the next section, which explores the diagnosis of FAS.)

FAS

The following are the most acknowledged and accepted criteria currently used by diagnostic physicians in the developed world. Due to the complexity of the diagnosis, the following information has been adapted from the CDC guidelines and diagnosis guide:

- documentation of all three facial abnormalities (smooth philtrum, thin vermillion and small palpebral fissures)

- documentation of growth deficits

- documentation of CNS abnormality.

These criteria are discussed in detail in this section.

PRESENCE OF FACIAL DYSMORPHIC FEATURES

The effects of alcohol on the developing fetus depend on the timing, amount and frequency of alcohol consumption by the mother. Drinking alcohol early in pregnancy may result in facial anomalies since this is a critical period when organs such as the brain and eyes are forming. While individuals with FAS often present with a variety of physical malformations or dysmorphic features, the clinical features most often identified have been facial anomalies. According to the 2004 FAS guidelines, an individual needs to exhibit all three characteristic facial features (based on racial norms):

- smooth philtrum (University of Washington Lip-Philtrum Guide – ranking of 4 or 5)

- thin vermillion (University of Washington Lip-Philtrum Guide – ranking of 4 or 5)

- small palpebral fissures (at or below 10th percentile based on age and racial norms).

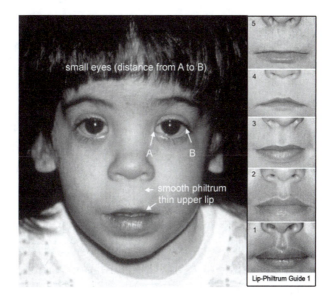

Figure 2.1 Facial image with lip guide (Susan Astley 2014)

These three features are not unique to FAS; thus, the process of differential diagnosis is essential in making an accurate FAS diagnosis. For more information about differential diagnosis, refer to Bertrand *et al.* (2004).

Lip-Philtrum Guide

The Lip-Philtrum Guide is a five-point pictorial ruler that measures the thinness of the upper lip and smoothness of the philtrum. A '1' on the scale depicts a thick upper lip and deeply grooved philtrum; a '5' depicts the thin upper lip and smooth philtrum typical of a child with FAS. This ruler, developed by the University of Washington FAS Diagnostic and Prevention Network, is intended for use by health professionals. Currently, there are two guides available for use: one validated for white individuals and another validated for black or African American individuals. The guide has also been translated into Russian. It is important to note that these tools are typically used as part of the 4-Digit Diagnostic Code system developed by the FAS Diagnostic and Prevention Network and used by many diagnostic clinics across the US. This tool was adopted by the developers of the 2004 FAS Guidelines because it offers an accurate way for health care professionals to measure lip thinness and philtrum smoothness, and it can be used in a practice setting with relative ease.[1]

Palpebral fissure length

Palpebral fissure length is the distance from the endocanthion (inner corner) to the exocanthion (outer corner) of the eye. In addition to having anomalies associated with the upper lip and the philtrum, individuals with FAS also present with small palpebral fissures (eye openings). Measuring palpebral fissure length can be quite challenging, and research on standardising these measures, particularly in newborns and children, is somewhat limited. Also, ethnic variation occurs in palpebral fissure length.

GROWTH PROBLEMS

While growth retardation has been documented consistently for children with FAS, it has not always been defined consistently. The recent guidelines (2004) propose the following growth retardation criteria: confirmed prenatal or postnatal height, weight or both at or below the 10th percentile

---

1   For more information on the Lip-Philtrum Guide, go to http://depts.washington.edu/ fasdpn/htmls/lip-philtrum-guides.htm.

documented at any one point in time (adjusted for age, sex, gestational age, and race or ethnicity).

It is important to keep in mind that growth problems occur for various reasons. Insufficient nutrition and environmental and genetic factors should be considered when assessing growth problems. The examiner should make sure that the single point in time when the growth deficit was present does not correlate with a point in time when the child was nutritionally deprived.[2]

CENTRAL NERVOUS SYSTEM ABNORMALITIES

More than 4000 scientific papers have been published over the past 40 years on the teratogenic effects of alcohol exposure on the CNS. Even so, the scientific evidence and professional consensus on the CNS criteria for FASD are not yet at the level of specificity that is available for physical features of the condition. The 2004 FAS Guidelines, however, do offer general recommendations to assist health care providers in identifying areas of abnormality most likely to be found in individuals with FAS specifically as they relate to functional deficits.

CNS abnormalities can be structural, neurological or functional. Documentation of problems in one or more of these areas is necessary for the FAS diagnosis. The criteria for CNS abnormalities are summarised below.

- *Structural.* One way structural anomalies are assessed is by measuring the occipitofrontal circumference (OFC) or head circumference. OFC is typically measured at the place where the largest measurement can be obtained. The health care provider should refer to the appropriate head circumference chart to determine the percentile under which the patient falls. The criteria for FAS diagnosis is one or both of the following:

  ◦ OFC at or below the 10th percentile adjusted for age and sex

  ◦ clinically significant brain abnormalities observable through imaging.

- *Neurological.* Neurological problems not due to a postnatal insult or fever, or other soft neurological signs outside normal limits

---

2   The CDC's 2000 growth charts should be used to assess growth. Copies of these growth charts are available online at www.cdc.gov/growthcharts.

(e.g. poor coordination, visual motor difficulties, nystagmus or difficulty with motor control).

- *Functional.* Performance substantially below that expected for an individual's age, schooling or circumstances, as evidenced by:

  ○ global cognitive or intellectual deficits representing multiple domains of deficit (or significant developmental delay in younger children) with performance below the 3rd percentile (two standard deviations below the mean for standardised testing); or

  ○ functional deficits below the 16th percentile (one standard deviation below the mean for standardised testing) in at least three of the following domains: (a) cognitive or developmental deficits or discrepancies; (b) executive-functioning deficits; (c) motor-functioning delays; (d) problems with attention or hyperactivity; (e) poor social skills; or (f) other issues, such as sensory problems, pragmatic language problems, memory deficits and so forth.

CORE DEFICITS AND DISABILITIES ASSOCIATED WITH FASD

Table 2.2 shows the core deficits and disabilities associated with FASD.

Table 2.2 *Core deficits and disabilities associated with FASD*

Functional domain	Characteristics
Cognitive or developmental deficit or disability	Specific learning disabilities (especially mathematics and/or visual–spatial deficits); uneven profile of cognitive skills; poor academic achievement; discrepancy between verbal and non-verbal skills; and slowed movements or reaction to people and stimuli (e.g. poor information processing).
Executive-functioning deficits	Poor organisation, planning or strategy use; concrete thinking; lack of inhibition; difficulty grasping cause and effect; inability to delay gratification; difficulty following multistep directions; difficulty changing strategies or thinking of things in a different way (i.e. perseveration); poor judgement; and inability to apply knowledge to new situations.

Functional domain	Characteristics
Motor-functioning delays	Delayed motor milestones; difficulty with writing or drawing; clumsiness; balance problems; tremors; and poor dexterity. For infants, a poor suck is often observed.
Attention deficit or hyperactivity	Described as 'busy'; inattentive; easily distracted; difficulty calming down; overly active; difficulty completing tasks; and/or trouble with transitions. Parents might report inconsistency in attention from day to day (e.g. 'on' days and 'off' days).
Poor social skills	Lack of stranger fear; often the scapegoat; naiveté and gullibility; easily taken advantage of; inappropriate choice of friends; preference for younger friends; immaturity; superficial interactions; adaptive skills significantly below cognitive potential; inappropriate sexual behaviours; difficulty understanding the perspective of others; poor social cognition; and clinically significant inappropriate initiations or interactions.
Other	Sensory problems (e.g. tactile defensiveness and oral sensitivity); pragmatic language problems (e.g. difficulty reading facial expressions; poor ability to understand the perspectives of others); memory deficits (e.g. forgetting well-learned material, needing many trials to remember); and difficulty responding appropriately to common parenting practices (e.g. not understanding cause-and-effect discipline).

These examples are neither exhaustive nor mutually exclusive. All domains should be assessed using norm-referenced standardised measures and by appropriate professionals using reliable and validated instruments. (Adapted from Bertrand *et al.* 2004)

When considering CNS abnormalities

Differential diagnosis of CNS abnormalities involves not only ruling out other disorders but also specifying co-occurring disorders. The CNS deficits associated with FAS, in particular functional deficits, can be produced by many different factors in addition to PAE. It is important to determine that the observed functional deficits are not better explained by other causes, such as organic syndromes or significantly disrupted environments, or other external factors such as abuse or neglect, disruptive homes and lack of opportunities. Obtaining a complete and detailed history for the individual and his or her family can help health care providers make a differential diagnosis between FAS and environmental causes for CNS abnormalities.

In addition to ruling out other causes for CNS abnormalities, a complete diagnosis should identify and specify other disorders that can co-exist with FAS such as autism, conduct disorder and oppositional defiant disorder. It is very important to note that a particular individual might have a conduct disorder in addition to FAS, but that not all persons with a conduct disorder have FAS, and not all individuals with FAS have a conduct disorder; thus, organic causes, environmental contributions and co-morbidity should all be considered for both inclusive and exclusive purposes when evaluating someone for the FAS diagnosis. Finally, differential diagnosis for the CNS abnormalities within the FAS diagnosis should be conducted by professionals trained not only in the features of FAS but also in the features of a broad array of birth defects and developmental disabilities so as to understand the distinguishing characteristics.

THE NEW DSM-5 CLASSIFICATION

A definition of neurobehavioural disorder as a result of prenatal alcohol exposure (ND-PAE) is as follows: ND-PAE is characterised by a range of developmental disabilities following exposure in the womb.

As a category in DSM-5 it applies to a presentation in a child or adult who has symptoms of neurodevelopmental disorder that is causing them difficulties in social, educational, occupational or any important areas of normal functioning. This category will be used when the child/adult does not meet the full criteria for any of the neurodevelopmental disorders in the diagnostic class of existing conditions (American Psychiatric Association 2013).

This is an interesting time with the DSM-5 recognising the fetal alcohol effect. As such, will ARND become ND-PAE under the billable code and, in doing so, help society to acknowledge what largely has been an unrecognised disability? A perhaps negative feature of the new DSM-5 is that it gives us many new classifications to describe children's behaviours, and in doing so even ND-PAE may get left to one side as a possible diagnosis in order not to enter an emotive diagnostic conclusion. If the physician can look at temper tantrums and class them as disruptive mood dysregulation disorder or refer to the defiant child as having oppositional defiance disorder, then society may not recognise the neurobehavioural disorders associated with an alcohol-exposed pregnancy. Diagnoses which absolve both the child's behaviour and also the parent's responsibility are not always in the best interest of either. A rush to the medicalisation of behaviours and a heavy reliance on psychoactive medications at the exclusion of psychosocial interventions runs the risk of developing addiction behaviours from a very young age.

Certainly, Streissguth and colleagues in 1996 raised the concern of children receiving a misdiagnosis. Concern abounds in the research world that children with a neurobehavioural disability as a result of an alcohol-exposed pregnancy are not diagnosed correctly. In many cases these children will be seen under more recognised and less challenging labels of Asperger syndrome, attention deficit hyperactivity disorder and obsessive–compulsive disorder (O'Malley 2007). Such actions of failing to recognise the fetal alcohol effect on the brain only derails the child further and speeds up their path to secondary disabilities with devastating potential outcomes for the individual, family and society at large.

These are still the very early days of the DSM-5, and it will be the direct experiences of parents, carers and professionals that will answer the question posed above regarding the future of ND-PAE. This is a seminal moment in the introduction of this new term and it is a dearly held belief of the authors that this may now help to identify FASD as a pervasive disability running through our society, and more specifically within our state systems of child welfare, foster care and adoption services. It is without question that the profession of social work has a pivotal role in the identification and management of the disability in order to better support the birth, foster and adoptive parents in providing care for the child with FASD.

Chapter 3

FASD ACROSS THE LIFESPAN

INTRODUCTION

As previous chapters have discussed, the impact of exposure to alcohol is different for each individual. Whilst there are some common traits or experiences, it is important to remember that this does not mean that the experiences will be the same for everyone. Impact on the individual will also vary due to factors including when the diagnosis of FASD was given, whether there has been early intervention from multi-agency practitioners, early childhood experiences in relation to meaningful attachments, exposure to additional traumas and abuse, and the presence of other co-morbid conditions which can multiply the impact on the individual at the various life stages.

This chapter is broken down into sections related to different parts of the lifespan. The early years covers birth to preschool, childhood covers 5–12 years of age, adolescence 13–18 years and adulthood refers to those 18 years and above. There is some overlap within the sections as the life stages are relatively arbitrary depending on the age at which a child starts school, progresses to high school or leaves school, which varies in different countries. There is also the overlap that whilst a significant proportion of those with FASD have been through the care system at some point, due to the unique level of their disability, some may leave foster care typically at 18 years of age and those with more recognised disabilities may stay in some form of residential support until a more advanced age which shapes the point at which the individual may view themselves as being an adult living a life by their own direction.

To introduce this chapter we present a case study based on typical incidents to highlight how FASD may appear across a lifespan.

Case study: FASD across the lifespan

Sheena had an unplanned pregnancy whilst she was a university student. Sheena was ten weeks into her pregnancy when she realised, and as soon as she went for the booking-in appointment to see the midwife at 12 weeks she was given a list of foods to avoid and was told that the occasional drink wouldn't be detrimental to the health of her baby, but to avoid drinking in excess. She decided not to drink anything during the rest of her pregnancy, altered her lifestyle accordingly and no longer attended the campus parties and gatherings that she had previously enjoyed. After a healthy pregnancy, Amy was born 13 days early but needed no treatments or interventions at birth. Sheena reports that Amy was a quiet baby but a fussy feeder and difficult to get onto a good sleep routine, but some of this she assumed was down to her being a first-time mother who didn't know how to help her baby settle well.

As a toddler Amy was constantly on the move and impulsive and seemed to have no sense of danger. Her speech was a little delayed, but when she gained speech she became a happy and engaging little girl. Sheena noticed the biggest issues starting at school when Amy seemed to struggle to relate positively to her peers. Whilst she was sociable and outgoing, the teacher noted that her social skills seemed under-developed and she was alienating children who were concerned that they would be in the receiving line for a bite or push. Amy had been known to steal other children's lunch boxes or 'borrow' things from other children that were never returned. It was assumed that with Amy being an only child it would only be a matter of time until she caught up and learned these skills now that she was at school and mixing with other children every day.

By the age of seven the teacher reported Amy struggling with some of the basic concepts related to learning and noted regular outbursts and general 'silliness' in the classroom. Classroom support for 12 hours a week was put in place to support Amy with her learning, but her behaviour still meant that playtimes and unstructured times were very difficult. Sheena dreaded when it was time for Amy to come home because Amy was so overwhelmed from the school day that she 'exploded' as she came in the door with shouting and angry displays of behaviour, and Sheena was never sure whether she could manage her.

At the age of nine Amy was assessed and diagnosed as having attention deficit hyperactivity disorder (ADHD) and over the next year there was some experimentation with drugs and dosage to find something that would help her sit still and concentrate so that she could catch up with her learning. Some of the ADHD medications had the opposite effect, so it was a tough process to find the balance. Amy progressed through school, and whilst she could sit longer in her chair due to the medications, she fell further behind her peers in academic assessments and she continued to struggle with anger and peer relationships.

At the age of 11 Amy went to secondary school and Sheena noticed that Amy's anger seemed to turn inwards and Amy appeared depressed. She didn't appear to have any friends and she would spend lots of time in her room. As the academic gap widened, Amy's self-esteem seemed to drop dramatically and she frequently stated that she didn't want to go to school. Sheena raised this concern at school but was reassured that this was in hand and that Amy was getting sufficient help for her level of need.

By the age of 15 Sheena thought that things were getting better for Amy because she seemed to have friends that she went out to meet socially and was making more of an effort to improve her appearance, whereas previously it was difficult to persuade her to get showered and dressed. The summer holidays passed without many concerns and Amy seemed to have a busy and fulfilling time going out with her friends. A few weeks into the new semester, the school began to contact Sheena with concerns of absenteeism. Amy said that her teachers hated her and she hated school and didn't want to go. Sheena tried everything to get her to go to school every day, but Amy seemed to disappear from some lessons, especially mathematics and science, and could be found hanging around town with her friends. When Sheena tried challenging Amy, it inevitably turned into an argument with Amy storming out, often not returning until the early hours of the morning if at all.

By the second semester the police picked up Amy numerous times with reports of antisocial behaviour, drunkenness and questions over petty theft and drugs. Social services were contacted, but the therapeutic sessions at the Child and Adolescent Mental Health Services didn't seem to change Amy's behaviour and she just agreed with everything that was said but didn't follow through. No alternative options were presented. Just before summer, Sheena was called to the police station connected with yet another incident. Amy had been caught in an act of theft yet was denying it. She had refused to say whether there were other people present, but the police suspected that the gang she hung around with had set her up, because the gang often 'used' people who were vulnerable to cover for them. She also had some drugs in her pockets, appeared to be under the influence and hit a policeman at the time of her arrest. She was cautioned and followed the restorative justice protocol, and was advised to change her friends. This was the first time that Sheena realised her daughter had been part of a gang.

Amy did not heed the advice from the police or from her mother, and after a string of further incidents related to offending behaviour and being drunk and disorderly, she became part of the Youth Offending Service. At this time a medical exam revealed that Amy was also 14 weeks pregnant. The Youth Offending Service had access to a psychologist who noted a number of brain-based skills deficits when Amy was assessed. Sheena was called to meet with the psychologist and discussed Amy's background and chronology. Initially it appeared that Amy may have had a form of brain injury, but when pregnancy was discussed, it raised a question over Amy having FASD. Sheena admitted that as a student she was drinking quite a lot but stopped as soon as she met with the midwife when she was 12 weeks into her pregnancy. Amy's baby photos showed the characteristic facial features of FAS and the growth deficits which were put down to prematurity but were now explained as growth deficits related to her diagnosis. Sheena was relieved that there was an explanation for her daughter's behaviours but was devastated when she realised that had she not consumed alcohol in pregnancy, this could have been avoided. At no point in Amy's life had any medical or educational practitioner highlighted this possible diagnosis despite the presence of facial anomalies, neurodevelopmental concerns and learning disabilities; instead, Sheena had been perceived as a young mother who was parenting poorly and had therefore enabled Amy's presenting behaviour. Of course, Sheena had blamed herself for failing to keep Amy from this path of self-destruction.

The rigid structure and strategies suggested by the Youth Offending Service worked relatively well for Amy, and her pregnancy progressed well. Sheena found that she had to fight for support services and raise awareness of this disability because every practitioner she spoke to had received no training on FASD. Amy had an IQ of 86 so she was not entitled to a social worker or therapist in the learning disability teams despite her adaptive functioning being particularly variable. When baby Ella was born, social services conducted a parenting assessment with Amy which seemed to be a standard off-the-shelf programme rather than one adapted to Amy's particular learning needs. Sheena had to take responsibility for ensuring that both Amy and Ella were given the care they needed. Whilst Ella is progressing well, and there are no obvious signs of FASD, the family has been told that with Amy's alcohol use early in pregnancy, they need to monitor Ella's development for later indicators of harm from alcohol.

Amy is now 20 and still living at home with her mother, who has to actively support Amy in raising Ella. Amy has been getting some therapeutic input to help her with anger issues and deal with her depression, which increased significantly after the birth of Ella. Amy is an attentive mother who dotes on Ella and there is a good bond between them. Ella is doing well at nursery school and seems to be making friends. Amy is looking to secure a permanent job whilst Ella is at school but can only cope with finding a part-time job because she realises that any more than that and she gets stressed and shuts down. She has tried a few jobs already, but because she has difficulties thinking on her feet, sales work has not been suited to her skills. She is looking at more routine work so that she can feel more secure and learn patterns of skills that she can use in the workplace.

Sheena is hoping that Amy will find a kind, patient man who will love and marry her because she is aware of how lonely Amy feels and how she would like to have a life much like anyone else. Support services are still limited for Amy and the only interventions at the moment are once-a-month therapeutic sessions and low-level disability funding. Sheena hopes that FASD awareness will increase the opportunities that will be available in the future for Amy and potentially for Ella if the alcohol exposure has led to brain-based deficits for her, too.

GENERAL DEVELOPMENT

There are many developmental tools, charts and guides that are provided from birth by medical practitioners which provide a baseline and guide to the child's developmental profiles. At the baby clinics in the first few years, and through visits with health visitors and associated practitioners, the child will be monitored in terms of their physical and developmental health. The UK Department for Education created a useful online *Early Years Developmental Journal* (see www.ncb.org.uk) which provides key indicators of achievement written in accessible language to help caregivers easily track and monitor their child's development. It is summarised into four key themes which underline key aspects of development: personal, social and emotional; communication; physical; and thinking.

Expectations of the child's cognitive functioning abilities may be difficult to discern, and delays or atypical behaviours may be difficult to recognise in the early years. While there are numerous developmental guides for 'typical' child development, other than the diagnostic data mentioned in previous chapters, universal guidance relating to the soft neurological signs of PAE is at times a little unclear for the caregiver who must then rely on comparisons against typical behaviour to identify anomalies. Table 3.1 shows a summary of development related to the stage of birth to five years from the Child Development Institute. This is a time when it can be difficult to identify neurobehavioural deficits as a result of an alcohol-exposed pregnancy; however, one of the consistent messages is that a diagnosis attained before the age of six years is likely to offer the best outcome for the child (Streissguth *et al.* 1996).

Table 3.1 Accepted norms of typical child development

	Physical and language	Emotional	Social
Birth to 1 month	Feedings: 5–8 per day; sleep: 20 hours per day; sensory capacities: makes basic distinctions in vision, hearing, smelling, tasting, touch, temperature and perception of pain	Generalised tension	Helpless; asocial; fed by mother
2–3 months	Sensory capacities: colour perception, visual exploration, oral exploration; sounds: cries, coos, grunts; motor ability: control of eye muscles, lifts head when on stomach; delight	Distress	Visually fixates on a face, smiles at a face; may be soothed by rocking
4–6 months	Sensory capacities: localises sounds; sounds: babbling, makes most vowels and about half of the consonants; feedings: 3–5 per day; motor ability: control of head and arm movements, purposive grasping, rolls	Enjoys being cuddled	Recognises his mother; distinguishes between familiar persons and strangers and no longer smiles indiscriminately; expects feeding, bathing and dressing
7–9 months	Motor ability: control of trunk and hands, sits without support, crawls about	Specific emotional attachment to mother	Protests separation from mother; enjoys 'peek-a-boo'

cont.

	Physical and language	Emotional	Social
10–12 months	Motor ability: control of legs and feet, stands, creeps, apposition of thumb and forefinger; language: says one or two words, imitates sounds, responds to simple commands; feedings: three meals, two snacks; sleep: 12 hours, two naps	Affection, fear of strangers, curiosity, exploration	Responsive to own name; waves bye-bye; plays pat-a-cake; understands 'no-no'; gives and takes objects
1–1.5 years	Motor ability: creeps upstairs, walks (10–20 min), makes lines on paper with crayon; dependent behaviour	Very upset when separated from mother; fear of bath	Obeys limited commands; repeats a few words; interested in his mirror image; feeds himself
1.5–2 years	Motor ability: runs, kicks a ball, builds six-cube tower (2 years); capable of bowel and bladder control; language: vocabulary of more than 200 words; sleep: 12 hours at night, 1- to 2-hour nap	Temper tantrums (1–3 years)	Resentment of new baby; does opposite of what he is told (1.5 years)
2–3 years	Motor ability: jumps off a step, rides a tricycle, uses crayons, builds a nine- to ten-cube tower; language: starts to use short sentences, controls and explores world with language, stuttering may appear briefly; fear of separation	Negativistic (2.5 years); violent emotions, anger; differentiates facial expressions of anger, sorrow and joy; sense of humour, plays tricks	Talks, uses 'I', 'me', 'you'; copies parents' actions; dependent, clinging, possessive about toys; enjoys playing alongside another child; negativism (2.5 years); resists parental demands; gives orders; rigid insistence on sameness of routine

3–4 years	Motor ability: stands on one leg, jumps up and down, draws a circle and a cross (4 years)	Self-sufficient in many routines of home life; affectionate toward parents; pleasure in genital manipulation; romantic attachment to parent of opposite sex (3–5 years); jealousy of same-sex parent; imaginary fears of dark, injury, etc. (3–5 years)	Likes to share; uses 'we'; cooperative play with other children; nursery school; imitates parents; beginning of identification with same-sex parent; practises sex-role activities; intense curiosity and interest in other children's bodies; has imaginary friend
4–5 years	Motor ability: mature motor control, skips, broad jumps, dresses himself, copies a square and a triangle; language: talks clearly, uses adult speech sounds, has mastered basic grammar, relates a story, knows over 2000 words (fifth year)	Responsibility and guilt; feels pride in accomplishment	Prefers to play with other children; becomes competitive; prefers gender-appropriate activities

From the Child Development Institute (see http://childdevelopmentinfo.com)

THE EARLY YEARS

Figure 3.1 shows factors such as positive, responsive care to the basic needs for food, shelter, sleep, clothing, consistent caregiving, social and family connections, friendship and love, which are all essential in developing a basic framework that will enable a child to thrive (Maslow 1943).

Figure 3.1 Necessary components for the overall health of a child born with FASD

Children who have experienced early childhood separation, trauma, disabilities or inconsistency in caregiving may also struggle to develop solid attachments, which can further impact on their neurological development and their long-term social and emotional well-being and health. Some foundational studies on attachment theory include the work of Bowlby (1951, 1953), which looked at maternal care, as well as that of Ainsworth (1963) and Ainsworth *et al.* (1978), which looked at the concept of a secure base. Mercer (2006) extended it further by proposing the internal working model of social relationships, which is the way in which the individual interprets their own understanding of relating to others. Main and Solomon (1986) developed Ainsworth's work and identified attachment patterns known as secure, anxious, avoidant, ambivalent/resistant and disorganised. Insecure attachments, such as the disorganised classification, can be evidenced in peer relationships being characterised by aggression and withdrawal which is often identified as 'fight or flight'. Children with ambivalent attachments are at a higher risk of internalising disorders, while those with disorganised attachments are more likely to externalise these disorders. As the theory and practice has advanced, the work of Dan Hughes, Nancy Thomas and others have advanced our understanding of therapeutic interventions which are particularly helpful for affected children (see, for example, Hughes 2012; Thomas 2008). When we pause to consider that disproportionate numbers of children with FASD enter the care system, it highlights how children may have additional issues related to insecure attachments which can run alongside the FASD and in turn exacerbate both conditions.

In terms of FASD, Chapter 2 outlines some of the facial features, growth deficits and congenital abnormalities that may be present in a newborn infant; however, what is also highlighted in that chapter is that many of the children on the FASD spectrum might not have any of those identifying signs, so practitioners may not even be looking for it at all, or specialist practitioners may have it on their radar and be adopting a watch-and-wait approach. This watch-and-wait approach is a typical course of action in early infancy, and caregivers and practitioners will monitor the infant and young child's progress against developmental and educational milestones and note carefully if the child is either missing their milestones or if there are any discrepancies in their development. Having clear early records can greatly assist a diagnosis for a child in later life.

Developmentally, babies and children gain important skills in the early years and 80 per cent of all brain cell development takes place by age three. They are gaining eye contact, forming attachments, communicating through babbling and forming their first words, learning to coordinate and sit up and balance, and taking their first steps. Much of the toddler years is also about the child beginning to learn about their capabilities, their family and significant others, and the wider social environment. They are beginning to make sense of interactions, patterns and rules as well as actions and consequences. These sorts of skills are recognised as developmental milestones. If a child does not reach these stages in a typical way for their age and early experience, this may be referred to as a developmental delay. If a child has persistent delays across a number of developmental themes, then they may be described by professionals as having a global developmental delay or disordered development rather than developmental delay.

Infancy

The initial signs and symptoms which may be associated with FASD are:

- signs of withdrawal, particularly if they have been exposed to poly-drug use which could include tremors, seizures, irritability, increased respiration and gastrointestinal symptoms (NOFAS-UK midwives guide)

- facial features, growth deficits, birth defects and evidence of CNS damage

- variable patterns of alertness (passive or over-active)

- irregular sleep patterns in terms of wake and sleep cycles

- failure to thrive and/or regular infections

- issues with feeding such as difficulty sucking, reflux, difficulty with textures, gorging on food, indifferent about food and bowel issues

- head banging and/or rocking

- gross motor delays

- absence of babbling, speech delays or unclear speech

- unsettled and difficult to comfort or having a high-pitched cry

- may not have typical eye contact and/or dislike physical contact

- unusual patterns of getting around such as no attempt to crawl or crawling on elbows, shuffling on bottom or up on their feet quickly and not stopping

- lack of response to pain or over-responding to pain

- over-sensitive or under-sensitive to the environment such as light, noise, touch and temperature

- continuation of the startle or moro reflex beyond 4–5 months old, not related to other physical disabilities or causes (Samuels and Ropper 2009).

This list of indicators is not exclusive to FASD and any of these symptoms warrants further investigation by those involved in the child's care. If an infant is experiencing withdrawal, they may be managed using medication and by being supported with cuddling and gentle handling in a quiet and less stimulating environment. It is also important to note that some infants with FASD may not obviously display any of these traits, which can lead to an assumption that the child has no CNS damage from alcohol exposure. For some children and young people, it is when the executive-functioning deficits show themselves in later life that a return to assess for FASD may need to happen. Chapter 4 provides more suggestions on how to handle some of these signs and symptoms that may be evidenced from birth.

EARLY CHILDHOOD

The preschool years are often a golden age for children with FASD.

(Buxton 2005, p.166)

As the infant ages, they may begin to achieve their early childhood developmental milestones, but for others there may be a continued pattern of lag. Some families say that it was when they were in parent and child playgroups, or their child started nursery, that they began to notice subtle differences that were not necessarily observable when they were alone at home. As was the case for the newborn, the consistency of carer and approach, having days with a sense of routine or pattern and providing ongoing assistance to guide and help the child in their development may continue to be very important. Some of the same concerns that existed in infancy, such as issues of sleeping, feeding and being over- or under-responsive to their environment, still may exist.

Early childhood characteristics may include the following:

- *Sensory issues.* The child may hate tags and seams in socks or only want to wear the same clothes every day, or may dislike clothes and peel them off at every opportunity. They may hate loud noises and cover their ears, not respond appropriately to hot and cold temperatures, be under- or over-sensitive to pain or dislike going places where there are lots of people or noise. They may struggle with toilet training and seemingly fail to recognise that they needed the toilet, or may be someone who cannot bear a second in a soiled nappy.

- *Food issues.* They may have issues with the textures and tastes of food, and have a limited diet or eat everything they see without ever seeming to be full. It is not unusual to hear that the child shows no interest in food and that it is a struggle to get them to eat.

- *Immaturity.* They may demonstrate struggles with understanding things that a child of their age and peer group may have been able to understand for some time. This may be patchy in that in some skill areas they appear bright and advanced, yet in other, seemingly mundane and straightforward tasks they have difficulties.

- *Tantrums and volatility.* The tantrums of toddlerhood may be continuing. Some youngsters may get overwhelmed by things around them, leading to outbursts or withdrawal. Some may go from 0 to 60 in an outburst and then it is gone in an instant, while others may appear moody and angry for days. Whilst tantrums and outbursts are typical for many children, caregivers often state that there is something about the intensity, frequency and volatility that is much greater in a child with FASD than other children to whom they have given care.

- *Peer relationships.* There may be issues that are starting to emerge with siblings and other children and their ability to play, share and interact meaningfully with others. In the toddler and preschool years many children can struggle with this, but for children with FASD, there can be a delay in their acquiring social protocols and particularly in understanding why their actions are upsetting other children or why they are being rejected.

- *Sleep routines.* They may have difficulty falling asleep or staying asleep and can have periods of being wide awake in the night. Some children may have night terrors or may be restless and move about a lot in their sleep.

- *Communication.* Some children may have no issues communicating or chattering endlessly in sometimes meaningless, continuous noise; others may show no speech, delayed speech or speech impairments.

As this section demonstrates, there is a great deal of complexity in identifying infants and young children who have had PAE unless there are the characteristic physical features associated with FAS that are clearly visible for a geneticist to make a diagnosis. The majority of the harm from PAE is invisible CNS damage which will rely on the assessments of medical professionals in partnership with the caregiver to begin to map the brain impairments and challenges for the child in order to understand where their deficits and, indeed, their talents reside.

One of the crucial aspects in infancy is having clearly documented evidence of alcohol exposure in pregnancy. This can come from the midwife, obstetrician or gynaecologist, for example, if those practitioners have completed an Audit C or some other assessment. The best scenario for the child is if their birth mother self-declares her drinking patterns during pregnancy as it will ensure that the child does not receive a co-morbid diagnosis due to lack of information. Individualised services must be considered to support the mother and her baby during her pregnancy. If she is living in a home environment where alcohol is part of the relationship, she will need different supports to a woman who is a social drinker and was unaware of the potential impact on her baby due to the mixed messages in the media. Birth mothers can worry that they may lose their child into the care system if they declare their drinking patterns, so it takes a lot of courage and trust in the professionals to open up. A non-judgemental approach incorporating motivational interviewing and practical support can establish a partnership between the birth mother and the practitioner which in turn will underpin the well-being of the unborn child. Intervening early can change the outcomes for that pregnancy but can also change the outcomes for subsequent pregnancies.

CHILDHOOD

As the child moves out from their infancy, they begin their academic learning at the ages of three and four years in nursery settings. Typical development suggests that by the time they reach four years old, they usually enjoy doing new things, play creatively including make-believe, enjoy playing with other children and talk about things of interest. They can usually say their name and follow basic rules of language and grammar. They have learned some numbers and colours, have a sense of time passing even if they cannot tell the time, can use scissors, can draw and copy letter shapes, and can play simple games. They can now hop, jump, stand on one foot, catch a ball and cope with basic eating and table rules.

Starting school is a big step for most children. It is a time when the child is discovering how to be away from the parents and relate in a complex and less predictable environment alongside other children and adults. With less focused adult supervision and a broader social circle, this in itself can create additional challenges for the child with FASD who relies on the prompts and instructions from an adult to help them understand and interact effectively with their peers in a given environment.

> Starting school as an individual with FASD can set them up for 'chronic failure and frustration'.
>
> (McCreight 1997, p.14)

> The common nurturing and stimulating classroom environment and decor can be the worst kind of environment for children with FASD.
>
> (Dr Kieren O'Malley, Knapp and O'Malley 2002)

Whilst some children with FASD are still coping well and developing well, this early childhood stage is often the point when traits and delays and gaps are more likely to indicate an underlying neurobehavioural condition. Some children with FASD may still be dealing with delays in their early development and display challenges related to sensory issues, sleep disorders, social skills deficits, language and communication deficits, emotional dysregulation, short-term memory issues and attachment disorders. They may struggle with physical activities such as jumping up and down, running and climbing, and may have difficulties with fine motor skills such as holding pencils for drawing. They may fail to understand two-step instructions or misunderstand words like 'in', 'on' or 'under', or others may fail to understand what the child says. They may have difficulties with social interaction and be too strong in relating to children or may avoid them and play alone. They may not be playing actively with their toys or amusing themselves and may rely on others to help them. You may find that development goes backwards at times when they appear to lose skills that they previously knew. Not only are they dealing with these potential delays, but this stage can throw up some new challenges for children with FASD.

OVERVIEW OF SENSORY PROCESSING DYSFUNCTION

Our senses help us to make sense of the world and our place in it. If the limbic system or prefrontal cortex is damaged, our senses are not able to send clear messages through the neural pathways to the brain so that messages can be interpreted correctly. Signs can include:

- unusually high or low activity levels
- over- or under-sensitivity to information from senses
- issues with the texture or feel of foods which makes them a picky eater
- sensory seeking and seeking excessive spinning, swinging, rocking movements
- sensory aversion to touch such as hugs, hair and teeth brushing, or tags in clothes
- getting over-excited easily and struggling to calm down
- getting distracted and finding it difficult to focus on the task at hand
- struggling to fall asleep and stay asleep
- clumsiness such as bumping into and/or tripping over objects in plain sight.

Therapeutic strategies

An occupational therapist's assessment will highlight what areas may be a particular issue for the child. Strategies will be identified for the unique pattern of traits of the child which may include:

- fidget toys to focus their need to move
- a quiet, reflective area to give them brain breaks or space that is quiet to regain composure
- deep pressure input or massage to allow for controlled sensory input
- ear plugs, MP3 players or sunglasses to accommodate environmental stressors
- movement breaks which give them permission to get off their seat
- natural soft materials for clothing, with tags removed, of a generous size to allow for movement, or tight to allow for sensory feedback
- heavy blankets, secure bedding or a sleeping bag, blackout blinds, a fan for white noise and so forth, to help with sleep issues.

Immaturity

What was acceptable and forgivable behaviour in the early years will become less tolerated in the childhood years by onlookers and this may lead to conflict and tension for the child. If children display impulsivity, tantrums, aggression, running off, immaturity and a lack of awareness of risk, there will be a mismatch between their advancing age and the expectations incumbent upon them. This is a stage where parenting skills may be questioned because the child may appear as though they have delays and have no sense of boundaries or have failed to be taught social graces. It is important to speak clearly to the caregiver and ask about their child rather than assuming it is a lack of skills and failure on the part of the caregiver to meet their child's needs. If there are significant concerns raised by the caregiver in terms of their child's lack of responsiveness to their parenting techniques and their concern that their child does not appear to be progressing well, then practitioners have a starting point to partner with the caregiver and look at solutions together. A caregiver who has carefully documented a child's development and flagged up concerns will have laid an excellent foundation for securing additional services that may be required. Also, it is important to remember that many children with FASD are working extra hard to follow instructions and to participate in activities, and some children may still be in need of a nap to recharge during the day, and this is particularly so for children who may also have sleep disorders.

Feeling 'different'

This is often the stage when a child begins to feel that they are 'different' in how they learn and understand their world and interact with others. They may find that their peers comment on this difference or act differently towards them, which can impact on their self-esteem and confidence. Learning more about their disability can help them navigate the struggles that some may face and may help to create an openness to receiving additional help in the school environment. For some children who are also in the care system, this sense of difference can be overwhelming and they may struggle with the multiple differences they may perceive compared with their peers.

Achievement

Whilst some children will be on a par with their peers academically, others may hear a pattern of critical comments about needing to try harder, even when they are doing their best. There is an increased risk of developing depression in this childhood phase and they need to experience praise to ameliorate some of the impact. Focusing on activities they enjoy, rather than on how well they are doing or what grade they receive, is important because their talents and abilities can be intermittent depending on how well their memory is working that day, if they have not had enough sleep, if there are too many distractions and so forth. Opportunities to excel in areas of talent will enable them to enjoy the sense of achievement that other children may take for granted.

Friendships

In the early years, children will begin to establish friendships with playmates that are positive and rewarding. As friendships and play become more complex and circles widen, some children with FASD may find that they are unable to understand the protocols and unwritten rules that are present in those relationships. There may need to be an active promotion of these friendships in order to assist them to be maintained throughout the primary school years. This life stage is important for the long-term well-being of the child. Streissguth *et al.* (1996) highlighted protective factors which safeguard the child which included having a diagnosis before the age of six years, never experiencing violence, having a good-quality home life from 8 to 12 years old, having a stable and nurturing home for 72 per cent of life and receiving early intervention.

When is a tantrum something more?

Most temper tantrums begin to subside when a child is around three years of age and their language and self-regulatory skills are beginning to develop. The presence of tantrums may become more concerning if they are happening a number of times on a given day, are occurring every couple of days, are lasting longer than half an hour and if the child appears to be unable to calm themselves and rely on the caregiver to regulate them. Furthermore, if the child attempts to self-harm, harm others or appears to over-react to seemingly superficial issues, or it occurs 'out of the blue', then these tantrums suggest something more complex and need to be discussed with a practitioner.

ADOLESCENCE

For most young people, adolescence is about developing an identity which is increasingly becoming separate from that of their parents. Social circles and relationships become vitally important and it is a time of developing skills and talents, thoughts and ideas, and coming to know where you fit into the world. This stage is challenging for any teenager, but for a person with FASD this can be particularly difficult to navigate due to the developmental delays and the issues that may have persisted from childhood.

FASD not only has an impact on the individual's medical health and well-being but also their social skills, how they relate to the world and, more importantly, how the world has cause to relate to *them*. Streissguth *et al.* (1996) identified a range of secondary disabilities that occur when primary disabilities are poorly accommodated including mental health issues, disrupted school experiences, trouble with the law, confinement, inappropriate sexual behaviour and addiction issues. These issues may become more pronounced during adolescence as the person attempts to find their place in the wider world and pull away a little from the direction of the parents. Those FASD people who have had an earlier diagnosis and earlier intervention may have begun to tackle some of the social communication challenges that they face, and their transition through this naturally complex life stage may be a little smoother. Additionally, those who have strong positive peer support may find that these friendships 'protect' them from trying to create friendships in later years that may be with people who are befriending them for purposes that are less honourable.

Disrupted school experiences can become particularly pronounced in these years if the education system has not been adjusted to suitably accommodate the learning needs of the individual and they are finding the gap between the learning requirements and their actual achievement beginning to widen. Additionally, in the teenage years there also may be less of a willingness to accept assistance and stand out within a classroom setting due to the peer pressure to fit in and be like everyone else.

The offending behaviour, or what may be deemed offending behaviour, appears to be particularly driven by the people that they are around at the time. The desire to please and fit in, the desire for adventure, their vulnerability, their lack of understanding of cause and effect, and their possible addictions may all be trigger points for this behaviour. Adolescents with well-developed support systems and positive peer input may manage to avoid many of the riskier behaviours, while others who have had less supportive structures may find themselves in trouble with the law.

The study by Streissguth *et al.* (1996) identified that over 90 per cent of people with FASD may develop mental health issues, and that the onset of depression is often one of the aspects that can trigger significantly during the changes they are facing in adolescence. For some people, the differences they see between their own and others' life chances may be a contributory factor, and isolation or loneliness may exacerbate mental health issues.

The National Institute of Mental Health highlights that there is a surge of the production of grey matter just before puberty, and in adolescence this centres on the frontal lobe and executive functioning; therefore, rewarding things can feel more rewarding and can lead to increased thrill-seeking behaviour that relies on the effective working of impulse control and the processing of cause and effect to prevent acting on those thrill-seeking behaviours. Steinberg (2005) suggests that by the person's mid twenties the maturation of the frontal lobe, including executive functioning, is complete. For our adolescents with FASD, executive-functioning deficits become increasingly apparent as they age from childhood to adolescence and adulthood, which means that they may face additional challenges as a teenager and their pathway through this stage may be far more complex than that of their peers.

Things to consider in this life stage are the following:

- *Academic support.* As the workload increases and becomes more complex, it is important to ensure that the correct learning support is in place. Have they a differentiated curriculum? Would it be better to drop one or two subjects so that they can focus on other subjects without getting so overwhelmed? If they are preparing for exams, have they got support to cope with the memory issues they may have?

- *Social skills.* Have they got friendships that will support them through these sensitive years? If not, can friendships be established by attending sports clubs, theatre groups, volunteering, neighbourhood activities and so forth? Have they been taught how to care for themselves and say no to unhealthy things into which they may be pressured? Have they had sex education presented to them in a way they can understand?

- *Personal care skills.* This can be a difficult phase for young people who struggle with their sensory issues. The physical changes at this time can mean that the personal hygiene and grooming aspects of life may be particularly difficult. If a routine is built in from childhood, the pattern of self-care may be easier to maintain in teenage life.

- *Typical teenager.* It can be challenging to work out what is 'typical' teenage behaviour and what is more an indicator of their FASD. Remember that this stage is a time of asserting oneself, challenging authority, learning about who one is and working out what one wants to be. It is a time of transition, emotionally, mentally and physically.

- *Children in care.* For the child in the care system, there can often be an additional challenge because transition planning commences whilst they are a teenager. Some will leave the care system at the age of 16 while the majority will leave care at the age of 18, although a bill is just going through in the UK to extend the care system until the age of 21. For those with neurobehavioural impairments and no diagnosis, the challenge of independence is going to be incredibly difficult. Best practice suggests that teaching adolescents to learn about interdependence rather than dependence will give them the best framework for support and a willingness to understand that few people really live an isolated, independent life, but rather live interacting with others and supporting and encouraging one another.

ADULTHOOD

Whilst the impact on young people with FASD is widely discussed and acknowledged, the research for adulthood has at times been less well known. It is for this reason that adult studies are more clearly referenced in this section for further investigation. This is the stage that can present a whole new set of issues for someone living with FASD. This is a life stage when the secondary and tertiary effects of FASD are more evident, as noted by Streissguth *et al.* (1996), with recent studies confirming their ongoing existence (Duquette and Orders 20133; Fagerlund *et al.* 2012; Rutman and Van Bibber 2010;

Salmon and Buetow 2012; Schemenauer 2011). Figure 3.2 highlights a typical adaptive functioning profile of an 18-year-old FASD adult.

Developmental Differentials

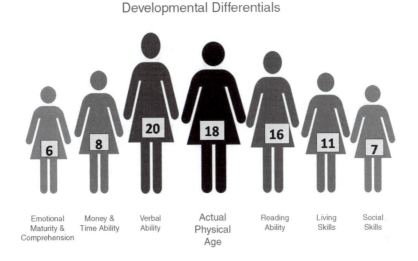

Figure 3.2 Developmental differentials in FASD
(Image created by Maria Catterick to illustrate the data presented by Malbin 2008)

While supports and services may have been patchy in childhood, many find that FASD-specific support can be relatively absent at this stage. Societal expectations suggest that adults will move towards independence; however, a growing body of research suggests that support needs for people with FASD may continue for life (Chudley *et al.* 2005; Jonsson, Dennett and Littlejohn 2009; Merrick *et al.* 2006, p.211). Grant *et al.* (2005, p.33) state that the quality of life for many adults with FASD is poor because 'access to services that might ameliorate their circumstances is either inconsistent or uncoordinated', often due to this invisible disability going unnoticed (LaDue 2002; Malbin 2002, 2008; Streissguth and O'Malley 2000).

Some countries may have dedicated support in colleges or vocational training, but the majority of adults find that they have to access mainstream colleges, workplaces, housing, community activities and general health facilities for services, and effectiveness of those services relies on the training and understanding of the practitioners. Caregivers often highlight that mainstream professionals fail to include caregivers when making decisions because their young adult is able to authorise their own decisions. This can have difficult consequences if the professional involved does not understand the nature of the disability and that individual's unique adaptive functioning profile. Particular areas for consideration are the following:

- *Employment.* Employment preparation training and employment schemes are an essential and supportive approach for work readiness. Ideally, there will be career advice in school which will look at strength areas and interests, and where possible, the young adolescent will gain slow exposure to the skills necessary to do that work both in terms of knowledge and practice to ensure that, when they reach adulthood, they have a chance of being ready.

  Streissguth and O'Malley (2000) identified that 80 per cent of FASD people diagnosed in childhood were living dependently, and 80 per cent had challenges securing employment. The studies by Salmon and Buetow (2012) and Duquette and Orders (2013) both highlighted that around 50 per cent of FASD people had issues with employment, which confirms that intervention and support is needed if the figures are to improve. One study highlighted that 34 per cent of FASD people were working full or part time, and 27 per cent were volunteering (Catterick 2013), which suggests improved outcomes compared with Streissguth and O'Malley's (2000) study; moreover, the fact that 61 per cent were doing some form of work, whether paid or unpaid, shows that many adults with FASD are contributing to the community. The issues that remain are that many adults find working full time can be particularly exhausting, and longevity in employment seems to occur when they pace themselves with only part-time employment in a supportive working environment. If the adult does not receive any disability income or receives only a limited amount to supplement their pay, then the stress level may be incredibly high for someone who is dependent on a wage to pay their bills and maintain their housing. It is imperative that a full assessment be made of the individual prior to employment and that he or she be monitored during their employment to ensure that they are coping and that any skills deficits, including social and communication skills deficits, are addressed to prevent issues from becoming so severe that they lose their job.

- *Housing.* This is a challenging area for many FASD adults. Debolt (2009) proposes that assertive outreach – defined as 'support that is proactive rather than reactive' – is needed to prevent issues of homelessness from occurring. Clark *et al.*'s (2004) study highlighted a need for affordable, safe and appropriate housing for FASD adults. Many adults remain at home living with their parents for extended periods of time, but those who have secured supported accommodation are able to live with their own tenancies. To make those tenancies work, there may be a need for help with budgeting, paying bills on time, maintaining the house, ensuring that other people do not use the FASD person's home for their own purposes and ensuring that the FASD person has a social network that prevents isolation.

If the FASD person is leaving the foster care system, they will typically be housed in flats with little aftercare support, and as discussed previously, their chronological age may bear little to no resemblance on their adaptive functioning. Many of the adults who seem to do well are often living in shared accommodation with friends, living with a partner or are visited regularly if living alone. Their ability to afford accommodation may well depend on their ability to work, which, as was highlighted previously, can be a particularly challenging aspect for some FASD adults. Tenancy agreements need to highlight that there may be issues with compliance due to the neurobehavioural aspects of someone with FASD. If the system is too rigid (e.g. 'three strikes and out'), it is probable that many adults with FASD will not be able to comply so readily due to executive functioning issues, and this can result in 'sofa surfing' or homelessness due to the perception that they have made themselves homeless through intentional non-compliance.

- *Mental health.* Most studies refer to the fact that over 90 per cent of people with FASD can have a mental health problem (Streissguth *et al.* 1996), which suggests that there may need to be lifelong support, understanding and involvement with mental health professionals. This is especially important when Merrick and Kandel (2007, p.237) noted that people with FASD had a ten-times-higher lifetime rate of suicide attempts than the general population. Many of the challenges to mental health occur because of the lack of compensation people make for FASD adults due to their disability being invisible and also because of the loneliness and vulnerability that they feel. Some adults may worry about what will happen to them as they see their caregiver age, and we often hear that caregivers have exactly the same concerns for their child. This appears to be particularly true in cases where the FASD person had been adopted by people who were already a little older when they took on responsibility for raising them.

> As they mature they may end up being 'a lonely child in an adult's body'.
>
> (Buxton 2005, p.175)

- *Behaviour and lifestyle.* Due to their often delayed emotional development, the behaviours of FASD people in adolescence may continue for some time, which is fine if there is little antisocial behaviour involved; however, those whose lives and lifestyle may be more challenging can struggle to stay on the right side of the law. Additionally, their vulnerability means that they are prey to being used for other people's purposes in return for an offer of friendship. If there is a police record for smaller offences in childhood and adolescence, this can mean that an offence in adulthood is taken more seriously. Stealing or aggression in a young person can be worrying but could lead to a custodial sentence if the same behaviour is conducted in adulthood. The justice systems are often at the end of a chain of absent or failed intervention to punish the cumulative behaviours which have arisen from lack of appropriate intervention (Abraham 2005; Clark *et al.* 2004; Lutke and Antrobus 2004).

  O'Connor and Paley (2009) highlighted a strong correlation between maternal binge drinking and alcohol abuse in adult offspring, and addictions with either drugs or alcohol can be particularly troublesome. Dual-diagnosis facilities need to ensure that they understand FASD in order to support their clients to overcome their addictive behaviours. The compounding of mental health issues and use of alcohol and drugs 'medicinally' to avoid other issues needs further exploration, but therapies that involve talking may prove to be less effective for a number of adults with FASD.

- *Parenting.* Many FASD adults have become parents, with evidence that a significant number are successfully parenting both independently and with their partners, and some are grandparents. There can be challenges for some young adults who get pregnant before they have reached a point of emotional maturity and have yet to overcome some of the challenges from adolescence. Adults with disabilities have the same rights in law to marry and have children (Human Rights Act 1998). This means that services would be expected to be available if they require support to parent their children and keep the family unit together. Many adults report that they are no longer caring for their own children because they have been removed and placed in the foster care system. This is a pattern that has been noted by numerous researchers (Catterick 2013; Clark *et al.* 2004; Denys *et al.* 2011; Lutke and Antrobus 2004; Rutman and Van Bibber 2010).

   Great caution is needed in assessments of parental capacity because if FASD is not recognised, then a lack of showing up to appointments or taking care of the finer details of their child's well-being could look like indifference or neglect instead of being recognised as a parent with disabilities needing additional support to parent their child. Parenting classes can also have issues if the training is not tailored to suit their learning needs and if it is not broken down into appropriate steps. Sometimes the behaviour outside of parenting can result in removal of the child particularly if there is offending behaviour or issues with controlling or aggressive partners, for instance. Safeguarding and social care and social work providers need to examine policies and practices to ensure that mentoring and support is appropriate to maintain the family unit where possible.

- *Skills development.* While FASD is a permanent disability, that does not mean there is no room for progress. Everyone continues to develop skills and acquire new behaviours throughout their life, and adults with FASD are no exception. There is growing evidence that in the late twenties and early thirties there is another transition point related to the brain, and this often shows itself in more appropriate skills and insights which can enable an adult with FASD to settle and blossom.

Appropriate assessments and interventions, preparation for vocational training, supported employment, informed justice systems, safe housing and a sense of community can ameliorate the effects of FASD for the individual and lead to optimal life outcomes (Chudley *et al.* 2005; Clark *et al.* 2004; Duquette and Orders 2013; Lutke and Antrobus 2004; Ragsdale 2006; Schemenauer 2011; Streissguth *et al.* 2004).

Chapter 4

TOOLS AND STRATEGIES FOR SUCCESS

STRATEGIES FOR INDIVIDUALS

There is no magic system or intervention available that will prevent a child or young person from becoming over-stimulated or that will dramatically enhance their abilities in the classroom or with their peers. There are, however, techniques and insights that can be drawn from research and practice for people with a variety of neurobehavioural conditions and learning disabilities that can be utilised to enhance the effectiveness of actions in relation to the individual and their environment.

Longevity studies on FASD suggest that around 90 per cent of individuals with FASD may experience some form of mental health concern in adulthood (Streissguth and O'Malley 2000; Streissguth *et al.* 1996, 2004). This suggests that attention to the health and mental health of the child and young person is important if there is to be an improvement in the long-term outcomes for those affected. Brain tasks that can be taken for granted, such as logical thought, memory, abstract reasoning, time management, social competency and other skills, are not necessarily automatically and consistently available for those with neurological impairments. This means that the internal stability that comes from a brain which works reliably is not present. The potential physical disabilities, learning impairments and co-morbid effects, such as hyperactivity or impulsivity, nutritional status, sensory profile, pharmacological interventions and emotional challenges from early childhood experiences and trauma, may also contribute to a destabilising experience for those with FASD, leading to potentially greater daily challenges.

Whilst physical and health-related matters, such as organ, tissue, muscle and growth anomalies, as well as pharmacological interventions, are managed by the health professionals involved in an individual's care, brain-based differences may have a less thorough approach. The brain-based challenges are different for each individual and may be evident in the way a young person behaves, learns (or does not learn), responds to their environment and feels about themselves. Whilst neurological and psychological assessments may indicate some of those impairments, much of how that is supported or managed relies on the resources, context and people around the individual on a daily basis; therefore, this chapter will examine a few key areas that may need particular attention.

Many of the tools and techniques have been gathered from feedback from parents, caregivers and professionals across different nations, and have been shared in support groups or in online discussion forums. Many FASD web pages include ideas for supporting the children and young people. Some of the most notable tools and insights are included in the work of Malbin (2002, 2008), Densmore (2011) and McCreight (1997), among others. The tools which follow identify a variety of ideas, but as each person is different and their internal world is variable, what works one day may not work consistently on other days.

PROMOTING COPING SKILLS AND POSITIVE ENGAGEMENT

FASD is largely an invisible disability, and the damage to the brain and central nervous system is not necessarily evident in any other tangible way other than through behaviour. This behaviour is not necessarily negative; it can simply mean an atypical reaction to the environment, learning or interaction with others which highlights that the brain is wired differently or the individual perceives the world differently. Individuals may struggle to have their needs met because others may perceive that they are 'forgetting on purpose', 'not trying hard enough' or are 'making excuses', and may fly under the radar of a diagnosis for many years or even a lifetime.

When FASD is discussed, often the more obvious or negative aspects of this disability are mentioned, which can lead to those much higher on the spectrum feeling as though they are being labelled unfairly and that people subsequently have low expectations of them. Whilst this chapter looks at different approaches, we do not use the negative term 'managing challenging behaviour' but instead use the term 'promoting positive behaviour' so that the tone is appropriate. There are significant numbers of individuals living independently, raising children, working and living fulfilling lives who have learned to incorporate a variety of personal techniques and supports that create a scaffolding for their success, and this needs to be acknowledged and celebrated.

Within the FASD community the term 'external brain' is often used to highlight the role of caregivers, mentors and support workers who guide and prompt in areas where the individual has deficits in skills or understanding; therefore, when there is a discussion of tools and techniques, there is an attempt to find ways to help the individual receive an external message that their brain ought to be communicating to them directly to help them self-regulate. It must also be borne in mind that behaviour which may be interpreted negatively is not intentional but may be a sign that their brain is not working coherently, their senses are not communicating accurately and the environment is not accommodating them appropriately, and what we witness is an overspill of confusion, frustration and exhaustion.

For caregivers and practitioners, a change of perspective comes when a young person finally obtains a diagnosis of FASD. What was perceived as intentional misbehaviour, wilful defiance and the challenging of authority is now channelled through the lens of understanding, and the emotional and psychological response to the individual's behaviour is different. Instead of consequences and restrictions and loss of privileges, there is a calm, quiet, measured and planned response that is about redirecting and resetting the individual rather than challenging or indeed conferring sanctions on the individual. There is also a proactive focus on changing the environment to prevent the individual from getting to the point where they are overwhelmed. There is a focus on skills and asset-based approaches to engagement rather than a standardised approach. There is a shift in understanding, and so there is a shift away from typical parenting, classroom or service-user techniques and a desire to obtain new ways of engaging with the individual to encourage climates that will promote the individual's well-being and positive behaviour. Fundamentally, there are three principles which form the bedrock of any practice: supervision, structure and support.

If an individual with FASD is supervised and there is a structure and routine to their day, and they feel supported through encouragement and assistance with daily tasks, then this provides a proactive framework to safeguard and empower. All the following tips, tools and techniques will only be effective if those three principles are in place.

GENERAL CONCEPTS

Useful tips, tools and techniques for interacting with an FASD person are as follows:

- Ensure that everyone applies the recommendations from the multi-agency practitioners who have conducted cognitive assessments with the young person.

- Be consistent in the way you respond. Use the same words, tone and actions to prompt them every time.

- Ignore negative behaviour where it is appropriate so that they do not receive attention for it.

- Some children will respond well with being redirected to some other activity, task or focus.

- Create a calming place where the individual can take themselves away from the situation to regroup and reset their stress and anxiety levels. It may be a comfortable corner or a space in their bedroom, for example.

- Thoughtful discussion is not possible when an individual is aroused and angry. Do not get involved in discussions; simply acknowledge that they are not coping or are angry and prompt them about how they can handle it – then remain silent or walk away if safe to do so.

- Find things to praise at appropriate times – even if you praise them for the way they went to a safe and quiet place until they were calm.

- Confabulation is when a person does not tell the truth because they are filling in the details either due to lack of memory or to answer a question to which they do not know the answer. Accept an answer of 'I don't know' to a question, because if you press them, they may make up an answer. Don't tell them that they are lying. Simply clarify and provide an accurate picture.

- Ownership is a difficult concept because it is brain based and taking things that do not belong to them can get them into trouble for borrowing and stealing. Continuously remind them what is theirs or put a name tag on it. For younger children remind them that if it does not have their name on it, it does not belong to them and so it should not be taken or used, put into their pocket or placed in their bag. If they take something, ensure that you consistently get them to return it. Until the concept is well practised, place temptation out of their way by locking away valuables and not leaving money around. (One mother sewed pockets up to help her child who particularly struggled with taking things to find less opportunity to do so.)

- Do not overwhelm them with too many choices. Starting in childhood, provide two options – otherwise, they may get overwhelmed or stressed about making a decision – and over time adjust accordingly.

- Progress can go forwards and backwards, so it is important that expectations be managed, and while progress is anticipated and encouraged, there is a need to allow for regression without criticism. Brain activity, memory and executive functioning are not consistent, and flexibility of approaches is needed.

- Thinking through consequences of actions is part of the executive functioning which occurs in the frontal lobe. Caregivers and practitioners often state that when they use 'time out' or consequences such as removal of toys or grounding as penalties to show disapproval of unacceptable actions, the child may not always understand and become angry at the adult who is deemed unfair. For some children, an immediate consequence with a calm, brief reason may be understandable, but this approach does not work for all. Adding consequences rather than taking away privileges may obtain better results for others. If there has been an angry or emotional exchange, wait until everyone is calm, because they will not be able to process what you are saying while they are feeling angry and upset.

IMPULSIVITY, INATTENTION, HYPERACTIVITY AND MEMORY ISSUES

It is particularly difficult for those people with FASD who struggle with these particular manifestations of brain impairments to blend with their peers. Teachers and caregivers need to remember that the young person is not trying to make their day difficult, not intentionally misbehaving or not intending to sabotage their own and others' learning or fun, and is often trying their very best to be like their peers and to please others. If you see behaviours that are not expected, stop and consider the physical environment (has something changed in terms of temperature, lighting, decoration, smell?), their personal needs (are they hungry, thirsty, tired or having sensory needs?) and the social context (are they lonely or overwhelmed by others, or feeling stupid or under pressure?), that their brains may simply not be connecting well and that everything is simply a struggle that day.

There are a few practical ideas that can be used both in the learning and home settings:

- Set up their home or classroom environment to optimise their learning or to calm them. (More ideas for this are given in the subsequent sections.)

- Check the fundamentals first. For example, could they be hungry, thirsty, tired or sick? The young person may not be conscious of this themselves.

- Allow them to use fidgets that help them to focus their impulsivity.

- Teach them to breathe deeply, use mindfulness techniques or count to five before responding.

- Ensure that there are not too many resources or toys out all at the same time.

- Use a talking stick or hand signals for turn taking.

- Use ear plugs to screen out noise or headphones to focus noise.

- Use overviews, outlines, prompt sheets and worked examples to introduce new tasks.

- Avoid over-stimulation from multiple sources of data and technology.

- Use novel, rhythmic and multisensory learning tools to reinforce the learning or to stimulate enthusiasm to learn new tasks.

- Invite them to repeat back tasks that they have been asked to do so you can check for understanding.

- Introduce only one instruction, sentence, learning step or concept at a time, and then check and reinforce before moving to the next step.

- Use concrete language where possible and be aware that they may take things very literally.

- Remember that for some children with FASD, the 'harder' they try the less they can do, so brain breaks may help switch them into a zone where they can think again.

- Tone of voice can be a sensory issue (for example, talking loudly may be perceived as shouting). Inflection and gestures may aid understanding to signify a question or to reinforce the meaning of the statement.

- They may need prompts and feedback to help them understand when they are beginning to dysregulate so that disruptive behaviours can be averted where possible.

- Ensure that the task they are being asked to complete is within their skill range and be ready to remind them and show them how to do the task again. Remember that previously learned concepts may not be retrievable if they are having memory issues that day and they may be telling you the complete truth when they say that they have forgotten.

- Using constant repetition is a key strategy to deal with ongoing memory deficits.

- The more relevant the data are for the individual, the easier it may be for them to recall and actively make a connection. If they love Lego, for example, use it to aid learning and explain concepts, and it will provide visual and tactile input too.

- Play memory games with pictures and objects to actively work on memory skills.

SOCIAL AND COMMUNICATION SKILLS AND SELF-ESTEEM

Children with FASD may be either quiet and withdrawn or friendly, outgoing and sociable. Commonly, however, they may fail to understand the protocols and tacit rules of social interaction and have traits of autism or even a full diagnosis of autism spectrum disorder. Social confusion or isolation can trigger low self-esteem especially if there are concerns about their ability to keep up with their peers. Families often share that their children frequently struggle with friendships in terms of making them or keeping them. Some of the issues with friendships are not that they lack fundamental skills to build relationships but that their sometimes unpredictable behaviour can place people at arm's length. Many individuals with FASD develop good social skills by adulthood and maintain a circle of supportive friends; however, for some, loneliness can be a big issue.

Therapists should be able to offer a range of interventions to help a child or young person develop additional social and communication skills which can then be supported and reinforced by caregivers:

- Access nurture groups and social skills training. Social skills training for people on the autism spectrum may be suitable or can be adapted.

- Augment speech with signs, cues and picture cards especially with those who have more pronounced language deficits and memory issues.

- Give them time to think and process what they want to say.

- Use every opportunity to model appropriate behaviour with other people. They may need to be explicitly taught about rules of conversations and conveying information.

- Rehearse phrases they can use to open or close conversations.

- Rehearse scenarios that they may find themselves in so that they are not overwhelmed if and when they happen and have a sense of what is appropriate.

- Circle time in the classroom can provide reinforcement of social protocols.

- They may not be able to understand and recognise sarcasm and take things literally, so careful attention is needed to the language that is used.

- Ensure that multimodal communication systems are used so that the young person is given instructions in a way that suits their learning style and understanding.

- Help them understand how to engage in play by explaining the actual and implicit rules that other children are able to pick up quickly.

- Provide opportunities to play games involving taking turns and use talking sticks to indicate when to listen and when to speak.

- Play may still be largely solitary in the early years because, as make-believe play becomes more complex, they may struggle with spontaneity that imaginative play requires.

- Teach them how to identify their own feelings, such as happiness and sadness, and how to read cues in others.

- Encourage interaction with your friends' children or with their cousins and relatives, and encourage your child to bring their friends over to play.

- Find out about local mainstream and special-needs clubs and activities in which they might be interested. Scouting and uniformed youth groups can be particularly helpful due to the formal programme and practical activities that they utilise.

- Sporting and activity clubs can be a helpful way to enable young people to build social networks. The best kinds of activities are those that occur beside others such as archery, horse riding, swimming and running, all of which foster camaraderie without the emphasis on intensive team interaction such as in football.

- They may have personal boundary issues, touch inappropriately and have difficulties sharing, waiting their turn, playing with others and so forth, which can create a distance between them and their peers. Whole-class education about inclusion and supporting one another and other social and emotional intelligence skills can enable resilience in the classroom that provides a safe, caring space for all regardless of their talents and deficits.

- A positive environment where even small successes are praised and congratulated can do a lot to boost self-esteem.

- Notice the young person doing things right, such as working hard, sitting quietly and trying their best, and praise or encourage them so that they know that you noticed.

- Everyone has strengths and talents, so giving them an opportunity to share those with others through writing, speaking, demonstration and helping can boost self-esteem.

- Encourage positive self-talk in all students so that they can acknowledge what they are good at or what they are capable of whether it is a hobby, sport, video game or personal attribute.

MANAGING CHANGE AND TRANSITIONS

Coping with change is an area which can often trigger an emotional and behavioural expression in the individual and become a source of frustration for people around them. Many young people enjoy the familiarity of routine and can become distressed if a plan is changed, an outing is cancelled or there is a different teacher in class. A brain that is typically wired can acknowledge a change, and due to the effective neurological pathways, available memories and calmer limbic system, they can process quickly that a bit of change is likely to be fine; however, individuals with FASD may need additional time to process this change to overcome their initial fight/flight/freeze reaction, and for some who display more perseveration and rigid patterns of behaviour, change is particularly difficult to handle without the following significant support:

- Ensure that they have a clear timetable both at school and at home so that they have a sense of what is happening and can mentally and emotionally prepare for it.

- Time can be a difficult concept, so visual timepieces, such as linear clocks and time trackers, can be helpful as well as verbal prompts, such as early warnings of change, to give them time to get used to the idea or finish tasks in a given time.

- Use social stories or role play to prepare them for big changes so they can work through the experience before it is real. Examples may include going on a preparatory visit to the hospital before they have an appointment, a visit to a new club before enrolling or a meeting with a new teacher before moving up a year. Such practices will create opportunities to prepare for change.

- Large transitions, such as moving home or changing from primary to secondary education or to college, are massive life events that require preparation in multiple ways. Ensure that where possible sufficient time be allowed for a plan to be mobilised, and if there are mentors available, get them on-board ready to support and encourage.

- Smaller changes and transitions may be managed by going somewhere when they are less tired, hungry or over-stimulated, and when there is something motivational in it for them such as a place they really want to go.

- If giving instructions, use their name, gain eye contact, make the time frame current and tell them what you want them to do, rather than tell them what to stop. Give time for them to respond.

DEALING WITH OUTBURSTS

The point that is essential to consider at this time is that these sorts of behaviours are often unintentional and are often a symptom of an underlying issue related to their personal, social or environmental needs. Traditional behaviour management techniques, such as reward charts and contracts, are less likely to work because of their impulsivity, the impairment related to understanding time and the sometimes abstract nature of the techniques. It is important to consider the following points:

- Prevention must be considered first. Is there something that you can do before they hit the point of an outburst that can help them regulate?

- Diversion tactics may be helpful for some younger children.

- What is going on personally? Are they hungry, thirsty, tired, overwhelmed?

- Does something environmental need to be changed (e.g. lighting, temperature, noise)?

- Would a burst of physical activity burn it out? Running, digging, sweeping and jumping may all be helpful.

- Is there a quiet space they can take themselves to or a sensory room that is full of calming lights, blankets and objects?

- Can you help them put words to feelings? Perhaps it is a frustration that they cannot articulate what needs to be expressed to relieve the pent-up feelings.

- Try to partner in the resolution where possible and praise them when they take appropriate steps to self-regulate or accept regulatory support from others.

- The tone and volume of your voice, your facial expression and your actions speak loudly, so be aware of how you are presenting yourself.

- Do not send them away for long periods of time to regroup (more than five minutes) as this may be counterproductive. They may not connect their actions and behaviours.

- Staying calm and walking away is a strategy that can be used for some young people, because if there is no audience, there is sometimes no reason to have a meltdown. If you do this, make sure that your child is safe and will come to no harm if their behaviour begins to escalate again.

- Consequences, if given, must be timely and simple to understand. Rather than being punitive and removing things from the child, giving them extra responsibilities to atone and right anything they may have done when angry may be more helpful.

- Always 'debrief' after the event when they are calm. It is often better to discuss it as a problem that needs resolving and work together on finding solutions to the problem. Never ask 'why' because they will often not know why and may confabulate to please you. Questions with a 'what' can often elicit better responses than questions with a 'why'.

- Remember that cause and effect is difficult for people with FASD and they may repeat the same errors again because of short-term memory issues or because the context was different and they were unable to transfer a concept learned in a different context across to the new context.

SPECIAL CONSIDERATIONS FOR YOUNG PEOPLE WITH FOSTER CARE AND ADOPTION EXPERIENCE

The following considerations should be taken into account regarding young people who have been in foster care and/or adopted:

- Remember that they may have broken or fragile attachments which will influence how they relate to events, how they feel emotionally and who they feel they can trust. Consider that there may have been traumatic events and experiences of violence or abuse in their history, so gentle yet firm and consistent approaches and active, attentive parenting will help build a sense of stability.

- If they have been through a number of foster homes, then it is likely that they may have been told that they are not trying hard enough or are naughty and disruptive. They will need to hear a lot of praise and encouragement and experience positive over-parenting to help them to begin to change their view of themselves.

- Their memory issues may cause them to forget a lot of facts about themselves or confabulate and fill in the gaps. Life-story work is very important for them, and practitioners and caregivers need to ensure that this work is conducted in a timely manner so that early childhood history is not lost or distorted.

- There may have been inconsistent stimulation or lack of opportunities for learning and development, so consolidating their existing learning and then exposing them to new skills, concepts and experiences may accelerate their capacity to learn and discover new talents.

PROMOTING PERSONAL SKILLS
Eating skills and diet

Eating and providing the right nutritional balance for people with FASD can be an ongoing issue. It is not uncommon to hear that children have little appetite and that food does not have the same interest for them compared with other children their age. It might be that they do not know when they are full and continue to eat until directed to stop. Whilst there is much that can be done to enable individuals to read those signs, ultimately, if their brain does not communicate hunger and thirst, then this issue can continue into adulthood unless routines are put in place which provide them with an external prompt. The caregiver should engage in the following practices:

- Look for any sucking, chewing or swallowing issues. Some children struggle to move food around their mouth easily. The occupational therapist will assess their oral motor skills and identify issues.

- Be aware that sensory issues can relate to how food looks, tastes, smells and feels, as well as the temperature, the presentation and even the shape.

- Limit the choices in food as there can be difficulty for some people to make a choice and they may feel overwhelmed by the options, the stress of which puts them off their food.

- Providing little and often, and allowing extra time for meals, may be helpful for some people as they may struggle to remain seated due to their impulsivity.

- Weighted lap blankets or chairs that give sensory feedback could be used to help them remain seated. Do not over-extend mealtimes if they are impulsive or hyperactive as they will fail to remain seated. Others will eat extremely slowly and additional time may need to be given to help them find the time to complete a meal.

- Remove unnecessary distractions and where possible always sit in the same place at the same table at home.

- Some caregivers have said that their children actually respond better if they are sitting in front of a TV because when they are distracted, they end up automatically eating far more food compared with when they are eating in silence. (Use caution with this as some children may be too distracted by TV to eat!)

Self-care

The sensory issues that individuals experience may also influence how they feel about bathing, brushing their teeth, what they wear and what fragrances they use. There is also a level of complexity related to each self-care step and this can overwhelm people who struggle to sequence properly or are impulsive and take less than a minute in the bathroom. Caregivers should maintain the following practices:

- Build good hygiene practices into everyday routines from an early age and do not deviate.

- Use wall charts, social stories and prompts to break down tasks into steps for completion.

- Keep all their washing items in one colour so they can recognise the things that are theirs.

- Try to find washing items with smells that they like or are fragrance free if they are sensitive to particular sorts of smells.

- Some children may not like the way things feel on their skin, whether it be a roll-on deodorant or a soap, or how things taste, such as toothpaste, so try different brands to see what works best.

- Use a visual timer in the shower to help them understand when it is time to get out, or place a waterproof tape line in the bath so that they do not fill it too far. Ensure that there is a thermostat on the water because some young people are under-sensitive and will get burned if they fail to recognise how hot the water is.

- They may need your assistance with personal care for longer than anticipated due to their developmental delays or fine and gross motor-skills deficits.

- Ensure that all clothing is breathable and has no itchy tags or seams that irritate. Once you find something that works through trial and error, it is worth following that concept with regard to all their clothes.

- If they have a particularly favourite item of clothing, then purchase a spare item in case one gets misplaced or damaged or to swap it when one is in the wash.

- Some children do not perceive temperature appropriately and in cold climates may be at risk of hypothermia if they have not been instructed what to wear for the day.

STRATEGIES FOR THE HOME

Children and young people rely on their families and their home life to create a climate of stability so that they can cope with being in the community, attending school, being around other people and reaching their potential. It is important that their home be a safe place for them to be themselves, relax, learn new skills and gain support, praise and encouragement that builds their self-esteem and counteracts the often daily barrage of negative comments that are sown into them from people who do not understand their disability. As discussed in previous chapters, many of the children and young people with FASD have experience of the fostering or adoption systems, with some having multiple moves of home as part of that experience. Broken attachments, early traumatic experiences, multiple caregivers and varying home rules and parenting approaches mean that, for some, family life may not have been easy.

There can be an assumption that children being raised by birth families may have a particularly difficult experience, but there is a need to acknowledge that many have been raised in fantastic birth families with all the security and love they need. This faulty assumption is usually connected with the perception that every mother must have alcohol-dependence issues if she has a child with FASD, which is simply not the case. In those instances where there are some birth families where alcohol dependency may be an ongoing issue, additional support and services need to be established to support the whole family in order to provide the therapeutic services that may be needed to keep them together and promote recovery.

Our environments can influence our moods in dramatic ways. In a room that is tense, we can find ourselves responding to that environment by becoming tense ourselves. Planners and architects speak about creating environments that are light and airy or cosy and comfortable to create a sense of well-being in homes or to convey a particular atmosphere in workplaces or leisure arcades. We have all probably gone into houses or spaces that we have been glad to leave because the decor was clashing or there were too many trinkets and objects in the room that left us feeling oppressed. Not all of us like the same environments, and one person's hoarding is another person's comfort in being surrounded by all their belongings. Whatever our perspective, we have the ability to adapt to surroundings and self-manage our behaviour if things are not to our liking or preference and we may make the choice not to return to somewhere that leaves us feeling uncomfortable.

This illustration simply introduces the idea that environment can influence us, our comfort levels and our actions. For children and adults with FASD whose sensory world may be over- or under-stimulating (and even both at the same time), this sensitivity to the environment can result in strong reactions to the experience. One young adult explained his experience as follows:

> The volume of my senses is turned way up loud and I see swirls and patterns on wallpaper and carpets as constantly moving and shouting at me to look at them. Then there are the noises of the ticking clock which pound in my head. Then there are too many people in the space even if it is just one or two people because they move and talk and make noises themselves which adds to the sounds. Usually someone has the TV on or they are clicking away on a laptop beside me. Don't even get me started on all the textures and the smells in a room from perfumes to old food to sweaty bodies...yuk!

Caregivers consistently report that simpler room decor with less clutter and toys and easy, clean lines can make all the difference to their children in lowering their sensory stimulation. With memory issues being a consistent problem for people with FASD, it is not advisable to change the environment very much such as moving furniture or redecorating frequently. Adolescents may enjoy creating their bedroom with your help and pick out the colours that help them to feel calm. Be aware that they may not pick colours that you would choose, but if their bedroom is to be their sanctuary, then what matters most is how it helps them to feel calm and safe.

This brief introduction to the sensory world of a child or young person with FASD can begin to identify potential triggers that need to be adjusted for comfort. A common phrase used in the FASD community suggests that we should aim to 'change the environment, not the child', suggesting that if the environment is right, they will cope better. The individuals may identify solutions themselves or you may use trial-and-error learning, and whilst there is much that can be adjusted in your own home, there is sadly far less control in the school, when shopping and in the wider social context. Remember that the overload can relate to something they see, hear, taste, smell or touch, or can be due to movement or their perceptions of where they are in relation to their world, so there is a great capacity for something to be irritating, distracting or overwhelming for the young person to whom you are giving care. The occupational therapist should be able to provide a list of possible suggestions about sensory interventions related to the assessment they conduct.

Home environment

The following considerations should be kept in mind when assessing the home environment:

- Create a stable routine from morning until bedtime, seven days a week, and try to stick to it.

- You may have two routines, one for the school year and one for the holidays and weekends.

- Follow a standard procedure for all tasks, from how to brush their teeth to clearing the table after a meal. The repetition of standard tasks will enable them to learn processes that will be embedded in their long-term memory.

- Try to identify the triggers for the individual with FASD. Do not forget to ask them, as sometimes they may be able to identify those triggers themselves but have never joined the dots as to how the environment makes them feel and react.

- Are there changes you can make to their home and bedroom to create a space that is calming?

- Can you create simple storage solutions so that they are not overwhelmed by their toys and clothes, and place them behind closed doors so that it keeps the lines simple?

- For the child that struggles to remember where things go, can you put simple picture or word labels on the storage boxes to help them return goods to their correct locations?

- Do they like small spaces? Can you give them a pop-up tent or a cardboard-box corner so that when they need to 'regroup' they can crawl into their contained space with blankets or music to regain their sense of equilibrium?

Sleeping

Sleep disruption is often reported by caregivers, and Jan *et al.* (2010) highlight that sleep deprivation exacerbates other areas such as cognition, health, behaviour and daily activities. If you are caring for a child with FASD, their sleep/wake cycle may not concur with what the experts say should be happening at their stage of development. Sleep/wake cycles are operated from the brain through two main chemicals called melatonin, the night chemical, and serotonin, the day chemical. This brain function may be damaged from prenatal alcohol exposure, and as such is not producing the right balance of sleep/wake chemicals. So as a parent/carer struggling with a child's sleep difficulty, or as a professional supporting a parent and child where sleep is a major problem, it is important to first determine what sleep/wake pattern, if any, is operating in the child. Are there key times or stages that seem worse than others? One way to identify the key factors is to complete a sleep/wake questionnaire to understand the issues before seeking a medical response to the problem; however, this is not always the case, and children may be given psychotropic medication for something that might just be relieved through home-based environmental tweaks or changes in the child's world. The appendix of this book contains a sleep assessment which can be used to identify specific issues that can then be followed up by a practitioner. Sleep disruption can be anything from struggles with falling asleep to staying asleep, as well as restlessness, night terrors and waking up tired. Sleep (or lack of it) is related to a number of issues including the chemical balance of melatonin in the brain. There are some practical things that can be done to assist with the promotion of sleep:

- Have a calm bedtime routine that starts early evening to enable their bodies to wind down in time for sleep. This can include baths, one-to-one time, soothing music, listening to a story and so forth.

- Decorate the room in a way that calms the child (e.g. through colours and lighting).

- Make their bedroom a distraction-free zone to help them sleep by removing technology and toys.

- White noise from electrical goods, the hum from fish tanks, bubble lamps and water features can soothe some children and young people.

- Safeguard their bedroom with window fixings that are age appropriate so that the child does not fall out.

- If they struggle with light or darkness in their bedroom, use a night light or blackout curtains as needed.

- If you have a child that switches the main light on and off repeatedly for sensory input, you can replace it with something else, such as a night light, or give them a little page light with a clicker so that it addresses their need to click something on and off (and it provides light if that is their sensory need).

- Keep a monitor in the room to hear them when they call or have bad dreams or need help getting to the toilet, or if they are struggling and may do something dangerous. (Be aware of the need for privacy for older children and consider alternatives.)

- Some children may prefer being tightly tucked into their beds using larger-sized sheets or sleeping bags. (Remember that it is not advisable to bundle up infants.)

- Caregivers have reported good results with weighted blankets that have been specially made for children on the advice of their occupational therapist. Do not use them if your occupational therapist has not suggested this for your child.

- There may be ongoing challenges if the child is sharing a room, and consideration may need to be given to staggering out bedtimes to allow one child to get to sleep before the other is placed in the bedroom.

- Hanging a drape or carpet tape markers may serve to delineate space to help the child to understand what they can and cannot do within that bedroom in relation to other children's property.

- Some young people have altered body clocks and may need pharmacological support to enable them to fall asleep and remain asleep throughout the night. This should only be used when standard techniques do not work.

- Try to maintain sleep patterns on weekdays and weekends to help the body regulate.

STRATEGIES FOR THE COMMUNITY

Some children and young people with FASD may feel calmer in open spaces with natural sounds and smells and space to breathe and move about, whilst for others it may hold a lot of fears and traumas about bugs and sensitivity to the climate and the sense of the unknown. Furthermore, for some children, going out means having to go on a car ride, and that can have a sensory overload all its own in relation to being fastened in the belt or harness, the pace at which the world zooms by and the additional noises and movement of people in the car. Some children and young people may enjoy travelling and find that fast movement relaxes them; they are the sorts of children who may spend time whirling and twirling, watching the washing machine on the spin cycle or enjoy spinning wheels on toy cars. One preschooler to whom one of the present authors gave care loved being outdoors and was a real 'nature boy', but when there was too much noise or too many people around, he would suddenly jump back into his buggy/stroller and pull the canopy way down in front of him so that he could regroup and calm his sensory world. He did not have language to describe how he was feeling, but the way he managed himself was pretty smart for a person so young. For the child that is highly sensitive to what they encounter, being outside can be challenging, and careful planning and strategies can make all the difference to some children.

The initial question is whether you really need to go to a particular place that triggers the child, for example the supermarket, which may provide particular concerns:

- Could you go there by yourself and leave your child happily playing with someone else?

- Could you utilise social stories to help them cope with the new experience? (Social stories are often used for children with autism spectrum conditions, and there is a whole field of research which supports their use.)

- Could you go for a short period of time so that they are not as overwhelmed?

- Could you go at a time of day when it is quiet at the location where you are going?

- Can you leave easily when you recognise that their ability to cope is diminishing?

- Have you created a strategy (such as a secret signal) so that they can tell you when their ability to cope is nearing its end and before their *inability* to cope results in behaviour that neither you nor they wish to see exhibited?

- Can they be put to use fetching the items on the shopping list to utilise their energy in a productive way?

- Would they prefer to sit in the trolley with music headphones to cope with the shopping experience?

- For a younger child, can you distract them with songs, snacks, racing the trolley or some other distraction tool that they enjoy so that they do not feel as though the activity is taking so long?

- Will they stay beside you when you are out for a walk or do they have a tendency to run off in outside spaces? For a younger child, there are backpacks with a walking band attached so that if they begin to move away, they can only go arm's length from you.

- Continuous repetition of returning to sit in the car or on a seat, or returning home if they are running away and/or acting dangerously, may help them to understand over time that if they want to be outside, then there is a particular proximity within which they must be with their caregiver.

- Sunglasses may be useful for children who do not like sunlight or wish to avoid eye contact with new people.

- Some children do not realise when they are hot or cold, so they may need regular prompts to layer up or remove a layer. Breathable fabrics help prevent over-heating.

- Some children may need to be prompted to consume more fluids to prevent dehydration when they are in the sun.

- Some children and young people hate being in a car seat and buckled up. Place some padded strap guards on the seat belt to prevent the feeling of them cutting into the child. Full harnesses may be needed for children who enjoy being Houdini and removing themselves from the straps. Additional locks which go over the buckle to make them tamper-proof for younger children can be purchased from motor part shops.

- Lap trays and back-of-the-seat storage can keep their toys to hand and make the journey pass more quickly.

- Does the child enjoy audiovisual resources to keep them stimulated and content?

For some caregivers, it can be challenging to go out in the community, so it is important to look for groups and activities which support children with disabilities because it is very easy to become isolated. Some of the most relaxing times can come from being around others who understand you and your child, and will understand if your child is having a tantrum or refuses to share or lashes out, without judging you on your parenting skills.

STRATEGIES FOR SCHOOLS AND LEARNING ENVIRONMENTS

The child or young person with FASD spends a great deal of time in the educational environment, so it is important that teaching staff have a clear understanding of the child's learning needs, strengths and objectives. In caregiver support groups, this particular area is one that is spoken about more than any other topic because of the specific challenges it presents. If the education support is individualised and child centred, then it can be extremely positive, but if there is a lack of understanding or a compromise between lack of resources and the child's needs, then life is very difficult for both the child and the family.

In a qualitative study by Catterick (2013), 85 adults with FASD were asked to reflect on service provision across their lifespan. One of the most emotive areas was education, with many stating that this was extremely difficult and at times a destructive experience. Largely those with a more positive experience were being taught in special schools and classes with modified learning environments and curriculum. It was also noted that a number of adults were homeschooled due to a lack of fit within classroom settings and found the experience all the more satisfying. The challenge in education lies in stretching a student academically so that they can realise their potential (IQ is not a clear indicator of potential), supporting the student to integrate well into the social setting and to partner in managing the neurobehavioural challenges they experience. The focus needs to be on how the child is coping in a 24-hour day rather than how the school perceives they are meeting the child's learning needs over a seven-hour day. If the child is having an outburst from the stress of school the moment they walk in the door at home, then something needs adjusting in their learning programme. The focus needs to be on the child's learning, achievement and well-being, not the school's perceptions about their abilities to cope with the child.

Whilst there is often a more positive experience in the early years of education where a child is based in one specific classroom with one teacher for most subjects and a nurturing approach, the later education years involve multiple teachers, rooms and a more abstract learning approach, which is particularly challenging for students with FASD. Each school, and indeed region and nation, have varying mechanisms for how they achieve positive outcomes for students with FASD. There are some great examples of specifically designed classrooms for small groups of students with FASD and other neurobehavioural conditions at the Right Program and the Bridges Program in Manitoba (Canada). Whilst that would be the hope for every young student who requires it, resources may be lacking for this to be established as standard.

Imagine the sensory experience of a school classroom which typically contains around 30 other children with walls and ceilings decorated with large numbers of colourful artwork displays. The noises of so many people in one space may be overwhelming. The clock ticks, the tap drips and the noises from outside the classroom or in the playground invade the inside space. For some children, there is the constant fear that the overwhelming sound of the fire alarm or class bell is about to go off and send them into fight or flight. Concentration can be hampered by what other people are doing inside the classroom and also by what is going on inside the individual themselves. It is not surprising that the learning environment may feel anything but suitable for learning. There are some helpful educational studies that can be utilised in this context.

Families may struggle with a multitude of issues to get the child to school, which may leave the young person stressed before they even arrive in the classroom. There may have been challenges with getting up, washed, dressed, eating breakfast, brushing teeth, packing their bag and walking or driving to school. Some of the support strategies can be vital.

Preparation before school

The caregiver can take the steps below in preparation for school:

- Ensure that you follow the exact same routine wherever possible.

- Have a checklist system so that the young person can start to learn how to manage their own morning routine. (This may only work for students who like school and are motivated learners.)

- If the young person struggles with showering in the morning, have them take a shower in the evening and get them used to having a thorough wash in the morning and using deodorant.

- Prepare school clothes the night before and lay them out in the order that the child will put them on, which is important for children who struggle with sequencing.

- Pack school bags the night before, after checking homework and the schedule for the next day, to ensure that sports kits are ready.

- Have packed lunches pre-prepared so that if there is a delay in the morning routine, the food is still ready to go.

- Have a breakfast snack ready to go so that the child can eat in the car if they have struggled to get themselves organised in time or do not feel like eating when they wake.

School breaktimes and mealtimes

These two points should be remembered regarding school breaktimes and mealtimes:

- Supervision is important for all trigger points such as leaving and entering buildings or classrooms, being in the playground and whilst eating lunch.

- Children are particularly vulnerable over recess and lunch breaks. A lunch monitor or play buddy could be assigned for a child with few friends.

Classrooms

When the child is in the classroom, take the following into consideration:

- Try to ensure consistency of teacher, approach and learning environment.

- Situate the young person in the most advantageous place for their learning needs, whether it is up front near the teacher, at the back away from distractions, in a carrel, at a separate table, with their back to the window or seated with the learning support worker.

- Allow fidget items and adjust their work station with appropriate desks and seating to enable them to cope with their need to constantly move. (The occupational therapist or educational psychologist will have some suggestions on this.)

- Some children may benefit from creating a cardboard booth on their table which can screen out other activities in the room at times of focused learning.

- Have simpler displays or covers that drape over displays when times of focused learning are needed.

- Build social cues into classroom dialogue so that the child is informed about what is expected on an ongoing basis.

- Ensure that learning is multisensory where possible to give the child the best chance of taking in the information. They are more likely to be kinaesthetic learners, so ensure that movements and gestures underline the message.

- If the young person contributes and gets the answer wrong, they should be praised for participating and making an effort or for getting part of the answer right.

- Wired communication aids are sometimes used for children with hearing impairments to help them hear their teacher more clearly. They also can be used with children who are distractible or over-sensitive to sounds. Headphones will provide a clear voice of the teacher and ease away any other sounds in the room.

- If the children cannot cope with the bells and alarms that signify the end of lessons, then some schools switch them off or use alternatives. Perhaps the child or young person can be warned when it is time for the bell and can use their ear defenders to mask the sound when it occurs.

- Ensure that classroom aides have the training to understand FASD and other neurobehavioural conditions in order to guarantee sufficient classroom support.

- Ensure that the child has a clear daily planner so that they are aware of what is coming next to help them with planning their day and coping with transitions.

- Circle time can be a little challenging, and some schools have reported success with using coloured mats that identify the space that a child sits in when they are on the floor. This may help with children who cannot work out personal space very well.

- If children need to line up, then it may be best for them to be at the front of the line so that they do not push others when they are feeling impulsive.

- It can be helpful for some children to enter a room early so that they are acclimatised before the rest of the class enters.

- A quiet space or thinking space may be set up in a corner of the classroom or in another room in the school so that when the child needs breaks to self-regulate, they can signal the teacher and leave. This space is *not* for punishment; it is a soft space that is nurturing and helps the child decompress.

- They may need to move more frequently than others, so they could be invited to help pass out resources, take messages to other classrooms for the teacher and so forth.

Social skills

Regarding social skills, the following points should be kept in mind:

- They may have personal boundary issues, touch inappropriately and have difficulties sharing, waiting their turn, playing with others and so forth, which can create a distance between them and their peers. Whole-class education about inclusion and supporting one another and other social and emotional intelligence skills can enable a resilience in the classroom that provides a safe, caring space for all, regardless of their talents and deficits.

- Adjustments may need to be made for school assemblies, concerts, joint class activities, sports days, school trips and so forth. Suggestions include having the child sit at the end of the row at assembly nearest the door so that they do not feel so trapped and can leave if they are not coping. They may choose to opt out of certain activities and join another class for a lesson where they can get on with homework or be a 'helper', which could build self-esteem. They may find school trips easier with a parent or trusted 'other' beside them. There will be strategies as unique as the individual, and all inclusion principles must be considered.

- Homework can be difficult for children who are exhausted after trying hard all day. If they have memory issues, the homework should not be new material and should review concepts that they know well for reinforcement of their learning.

- They may need to be given regular snacks and breaks throughout the day and monitored to ensure that they eat their lunch and are not overly hungry, which would affect their behaviour and capacity to learn.

- Consider allowing them to head to the changing rooms slightly earlier or provide them with assistance to get changed for sports lessons, as they may not have the skills to do this swiftly and will be set up for ridicule or being told off for distracted behaviour.

- They may benefit from leaving classes or entering classes a little earlier to avoid the noise and busy crush in corridors, which would be difficult for those with sensory challenges.

- If classes are to be covered by a different teacher, then the young person may need to be told in advance, and their learning needs should be identified to the stand-in teacher, if possible. This may be a stressful experience for the young person, who may achieve less work and be more reactive. A classroom aide or assistant may need to take a more active role in enabling them to cope by offering more support, increasing breaks and supervising them throughout the day.

Numeracy skills and concepts

People with FASD often have challenges with mathematics and abstract concepts due to the nature of the damage in the brain. While some people may struggle with this all their lives, for many it will take a more focused approach and additional time to provide them with the tools to learn. Helpful tips are as follows:

- Make the concepts as concrete as possible and use tangible objects in the early stages.

- For some students, using linear time pieces helps them understand the passing of time. You can also chain together objects and remove one at a time to show time passing. Time trackers and egg timers also give visual indicators of time.

- Teach time by association, for example by relating it to events, such as their favourite TV programmes, or by meals.

- Use a digital watch or mobile phone and set alarms to indicate the beginning and end of activities. This is especially useful for adults who have to attend appointments independently.

- Use songs and rhymes and music, as it engages a different part of the brain that may be less affected and supports their understanding as well as aids memory retention.

- Teach concepts through multisensory learning where possible and use physical movement to help acquire skills (much like we use fingers to count as a physical act to signify a less concrete concept).

- Use real-life scenarios in school, at home and in the community to reinforce learning so that things are less abstract.

- Story sacks are a great way to make concepts come alive. Story sacks usually contain the book and all the items mentioned in the book to touch, feel and use to connect solidly to the story. The range of books is endless and it is a simple way to bring a sense of fun and interest.

- Money skills can be particularly challenging due to the often abstract nature. The FASD person may perceive three low-value coins as holding more value collectively than one coin of greater total value, simply because there are more of the low-value coins. Start early on these concepts and use repetition.

- Budgets are a particularly difficult issue for adolescents and adults because it involves executive functioning skills and mathematics skills to budget successfully. Find a system that works for them, whether it be that all money is paid into the bank to cover their bills and they get a small allowance to spend how they want, or that they have a nominated person to assist.

STRATEGIES FOR WORKING ENVIRONMENTS

This section is of particular relevance to the young adults and adults with FASD as well as to the practitioners and caregivers who are helping people with FASD plan meaningfully for their future. The early studies (Streissguth 1997, Streissguth *et al.* 1996) highlighted that the majority of people with FASD would struggle to secure stable employment in adulthood and identified that the work they do obtain may last relatively short periods of time. Schemenauer (2011) has looked at the workplace in more depth and identified the need for correct workplace training. A brief study by Catterick (2013) highlighted that whilst the struggle to gain employment may still exist, there are fewer people who are permanently unemployed and a significant proportion are enjoying a great deal of success and fulfilment in the workplace. Lessons gained from many sources suggest that part-time work is of particular merit for adults as they do not get so exhausted by the demands of the workplace. Many adults spend hours volunteering in the community and are using that opportunity to hone vocational as well as social and life skills. More frequently, adults are using their talents as their form of employment such as hand crafts, animal care, speaking engagements, writing books and, of course, homemakers.

Some of the skills and techniques for success in the workplace will need to be started in adolescence, if not sooner, to give them a chance to be embedded. Some of the basic skills will be managing time, mastering independent travel, understanding their skills and support needs, dealing with social environments and pacing themselves. The following points are noteworthy:

- Start identifying early the talents and skills of people with FASD so that they can become aware of the unique contribution they can make and the careers for which they may be suited.

- Some young adults will be planning to attend university and will have success in academic fields, but others will need to gain access to vocational programmes in schools, if their talents are more practical, in order to get them work ready.

- Build in life skills of getting up and ready within a given time frame so that they can be reliable in the workplace.

- Ask employment brokers and mentors to secure some work experience for them and to look at vocational skills that can be developed.

- Employment brokers and mentors may also be able to go into jobs and negotiate work trials with the employer, look at tasks that would be undertaken so that they can break them down into bite-sized tasks and accompany them in the workplace until they feel more confident.

- Remember that part-time employment is as much as some people can manage due to the additional cognitive effort and energy it may take for them to do their work. Ensure that they are not pressed to give more, because it may put their job in jeopardy if it becomes too much.

- Ensure that the employer maintains schedules and tasks without too much variation; otherwise, this can be difficult to handle. If changes are made, employees need to understand that it will be challenging for the individual, and patience may be required until they are able to cope.

- Help the individual find a job that suits their body clock. If he or she is an early riser, find a job that starts early, and if they are awake most nights, try to find a job that consists of night shifts. It is easier to go along with their body clock so that they are more productive.

- We may start to see opportunities opening up for some of our adults in supported self-employment. If they have creative talents and make items for sale, or are musicians, artists, photographers, writers and so on, then trying to help them sell their resources may be a worthwhile step.

The days of formal, inflexible working patterns need to be cast aside and employment needs to be rethought to enable individuals with FASD to find a work path that matches their skills.

Chapter 5

SUPPORTS AND SERVICES

There is a twin-track approach for intervention consisting of multi-disciplinary assessments and input from practitioners as well as lifestyle and practical tools used by families and caregivers. It is this child-centred partnership approach between practitioner and caregiver that will produce the best long-term outcomes for the child and their family. There may be tensions in the relationship which may need to be overcome but are typically due to a lack of resources, funding and staff turnover, as well as caregivers potentially struggling with the daily challenges, sleeplessness and lack of services who may have encountered numerous untrained practitioners proposing yet another 'reward chart technique' for them to try. Clear understanding of the family context and the child's needs, and the remit of the specialists and practitioners involved, will result in clearer and more supportive interventions.

SPECIALISTS AND PRACTITIONERS

A significant indicator of a person's needs and appropriate interventions will come from diagnostic assessments and reports from a variety of practitioners that may be involved in the physical, emotional and practical care of the child or young person. Knowledge of FASD varies between practitioners, ranging from intensive specialist courses on FASD to no exposure or training in relation to this field at all. Until FASD training is embedded in all practitioner and academic training programmes across the disciplines, caregivers and individuals will continue to be frustrated about being referred to a practitioner who has less knowledge than they have about FASD (which leaves them having to explain the disability and the impact to the practitioner). Whilst explaining on a one-off occasion is understandable, the multidisciplinary approach necessary for the well-being of those affected by FASD may place caregivers and individuals in the path of many different practitioners who fail to have a clear understanding of this disability, and they can get weary or frustrated with having to repeat themselves or simply being told, 'You are doing a good job, carry on, I have nothing more to add.' That said, there is an emerging presence of FASD training within the voluntary and community sector as well as field-specific academic specialities, so it is hoped that a lack of awareness of FASD may become a diminishing reality in the future.

Key practitioners can include the following:

- *Geneticist.* A geneticist report identifies the specific diagnosis of FASD and any other genetic concerns. Some geneticists will confirm FAS due only to its clear presence in the diagnostic manual (DSM-5), so it may be necessary to look at a confirmation of other forms of FASD from specialist diagnostic clinics if they are available and affordable.

- *Neuro-psychologist/psychologist.* A variety of tools are available to assess how the brain is working and areas of impairment. All children with FASD will typically receive cognitive assessments, such as the Wechsler Intelligence Scale for Children IV, which establishes baselines of functioning. A common assessment that is valuable for its practical application is the Vineland Adaptive Behavior Scale (VABS), which looks at how the individual can function within their environment.

- *Occupational therapist.* They conduct a variety of assessments to identify developmental coordination disorders and sensory integration issues, and they look at daily living skills.

- *Physiotherapist.* Their assessments and interventions support those who have physical impacts from alcohol exposure and seek to promote all aspects of mobility.

- *GP and paediatrician.* They track the overall medical and health needs of the child, coordinate referrals and discuss medication needs.

- *Speech and language therapist.* They assist with expressive and receptive language issues, social communication development and oral-motor skills.

- *Nutritionist.* They help with ensuring a healthy, balanced diet and advise on strategies related to sensory issues, drooling, vitamin deficiencies and percutaneous endoscopic gastrostomy feeding, among other fields of expertise.

- *Educational psychologist and coordinator of special educational needs.* They lead on identifying the individual's academic support needs, individual education plans and educational statements, and arrange for one-to-one support in the classroom or placement in a special school environment. The educational psychologist also is able to identify specific learning disabilities.

- *Child and adolescent mental health therapist.* They work with children and their families to look at behavioural strategies and interventions, parenting techniques, sleep issues, mental health concerns and attachment therapies, as well as other areas of well-being. They also conduct a variety of assessments to establish diagnoses.

- *Social worker.* They hold the history and chronology of the child or young person and may hold documentary evidence of alcohol exposure in pregnancy. The chronology should provide data regarding the nurturing environment and the traumas that a child may have been exposed to, and also they know how many placements a child may have been through since coming into the care system. They also can secure additional referrals to services and provide short break and respite care for caregivers. For adults with FASD, they also make decisions about transitions to independent or supported accommodation.

There are many other practitioners, including midwives, health visitors, ophthalmologists, audiologists, orthopaedic surgeons, asthma and allergy practitioners, dental technicians and specialists for specific physical issues (e.g. heart specialists), that may become part of the therapeutic team depending on the individual's specific needs. There also may be community-based practitioners such as early years' groups, respite carers, one-to-one workers and disability-specific support groups.

The list of potential practitioners is extensive, and for families who have a child with particularly complex needs, there can be a considerable amount of appointments and check-ups that will become part of their life. A practice that appears to be having a great deal of success is the case review or team-around-the-family approach, also known as the team-around-the-child approach. This places the family at the centre, and an advocate working on behalf of the family calls meetings and invites all related practitioners around the table to review the family's needs. This process can provide everyone with a clear insight into gaps and priorities, and it saves the family repeating themselves numerous times with every practitioner they visit. Some providers use a practice known as 'health passports', which can be paper and electronic case notes, so that all up-to-date details related to the child and family are easy to access.

An important point to note is that not all practitioners need to be involved all of the time, and sometimes practitioners get to the end of what their field of specialism can offer. Being open and honest about this fact can prevent the frustrations that can occur if there is a difference of expectations and a lack of visible progress. An ongoing area of concern is when families or individuals are continually signposted to providers but fail to secure services. FASD is a complex disability with multiple overlapping traits, and it is not uncommon to be passed between learning disability, mental health, addictions, trauma, attachment disorder, brain injury and specific-disability providers (autism, attention deficit hyperactivity disorder, etc.) and still receive no services because the complexity is unfamiliar to practitioners. The team-around-the-family approach can ensure that there are multimodal interventions in place and that gaps in services are quickly addressed.

It is also important to note that in some regions and nations there is a wealth of expertise among practitioners who have attended specialist training and are conducting world-leading research which examines the effectiveness of approaches and interventions for children and families affected by FASD. Much of the published research in FASD is conducted by committed individuals who are determined to improve the lives of others. It is not unusual to hear of parents paying privately and travelling long distances to gain the right services for their family. There are some states, provinces, counties, regions or districts that have specific mechanisms for referrals which can result in a 'postcode lottery' in which one locality has a great deal of expertise and services available whilst a locality just a few miles away may have nothing. The boundaries for eligibility mean that a family may not be permitted to cross into another district for services. There are also differences in who is funding the services, and whilst some central governments have a strategy document and provide a level of funding to secure FASD-related services, others may be operating with no national strategy, no central funding and few localised services. The UK, as an example, has only one FASD diagnostic centre to service the whole country in comparison with the province of Alberta in Canada which has 24 centres to service a population of 3.6 million. There is recognition, therefore, that availability of support and services is not necessarily straightforward, nor are they always funded, so families may have to access general services and navigate their way through an uncoordinated approach until they secure the assessments and resources that they believe are beneficial for their child.

The specialists involved in the assessments and reviews of the individuals or families often write complex reports using field-specific language and terminology which can be a barrier to understanding. The development of a clear and accessible summarised account of the findings written in layman's terms is worth consideration in every report by every practitioner. This is especially important when a report needs to be given to parents who may have their own level of learning disability or is given to adults with FASD who may need to understand clearly their own results in order to advocate for themselves in daily life.

An important point to note is that there can be a tendency to establish programmes or interventions which seek to 'fix' concerns or behaviours, but the focus needs to be redirected on strategies to enable people to achieve their individual potential. Whilst certain interventions and services may ameliorate the primary, secondary and tertiary effects resulting from the prenatal alcohol exposure (PAE), FASD is a permanent disability with lifelong implications, and a long-term service point is helpful for adults to return to as often as they need.

SUPPORT FOR CAREGIVERS AND FAMILIES

Whilst it is the child, young person or adult that has individual impacts from the PAE, it is the whole family that experiences the impact of this disability, and a focus on holistic support should be considered. Families may welcome the opportunity for counselling and therapeutic input to help them deal with the diagnosis and prepare for the challenges that their child may face in life. This may be particularly helpful when we consider the emotional impact for some birth families when there is a realisation that this disability was potentially preventable. As has been noted previously in this book, children with FASD are over-represented in the care system, which suggests that birth families may experience a separation from their child. Whilst the child enters the foster care or adoption system, at times the needs of the birth parent can be overlooked and it is important to ensure that they are also supported at this time in order to decrease the risk of further alcohol-exposed pregnancies. Support can include the allocation of a mentor, an alcohol worker, a counsellor or even a social worker who understands the experiences of the birth mother and can provide some emotional and practical support to cope with their loss and to help them navigate the complexities of ongoing contact.

If a child does not have a diagnosis and is being given care by a foster carer or adopter who has not been given any information or training on FASD, the caregiver may perceive that the child is wilfully disobedient, oppositional and defiant. The resulting consequences to the behaviour given by the caregiver may not be given in a way that the child can understand, thereby escalating behaviours and creating a vicious circle. Furthermore, the caregiver may come to believe that they are not suitably skilled to give care to the child because what they are trying does not appear to be working, and therefore they are failing the child or are being rejected as a parenting figure. This lack of a strong bond can result in questioning whether the child has an attachment disorder. Without appropriate information and services, as well as practitioner and peer support, this can account for children with FASD experiencing multiple moves, or permanency and adoption placements breaking down. Comprehensive training and access to clear chronologies and assessments will enable a caregiver to tailor their strategies and understand the triggers for the child or children in their care.

Caregiver burnout can be high when caring for children with a broad range of neurobehavioural conditions, and this is especially true when caregivers do not have a diagnosis to explain why their typical parenting strategies fail to work. A diagnosis can help to reframe expectations and enable greater levels of understanding; however, the additional attention to managing the environment and supervising the child at all times will still be time-consuming and can be exhausting in some instances. To counteract this, it is important to consider the provision of an ongoing package of outreach and respite care to ensure longevity of the relationship between the child or young person and their caregiver. If the caregiver is resilient, it will boost the child's resilience.

Key ingredients for building resilient families are:

- clear diagnosis, chronology and a range of assessments showing individual strengths and deficits

- coordinated approaches by FASD-informed professionals

- modified environments and activities to promote fun and success

- respite care and short-break care to prevent caregiver burnout

- timely responses by professionals who believe the caregiver or the individual with FASD about the issues they are facing and put services in place promptly.

Chapter 6

FUTURE POLICY AND PRACTICE

Throughout this book there has been an exploration of the nature of FASD across the lifespan, including how it is identified and diagnosed whilst utilising tools that support the individual and the family. Should the book end there, it would leave a number of questions unexplored which families and practitioners consistently wrestle through in looking for answers. These questions include the following:

- Why are we not preventing this leading cause of intellectual disability in the Western world?

- Why are we consigning this pervasive and destructive disability to the shadows in our society?

- Why are public health departments not delivering universal prevention messages?

There are no easy answers to these questions, and whilst some families and professionals have waited for government responses and 'the cavalry to arrive', there is a realisation that everyone must play their part to raise awareness of the disability, support the individuals and families that are affected and do everything they can to prevent further alcohol-exposed pregnancies. The *Parable of the River* is an allegory that illustrates clearly the need to continue to ask questions and explore what lies behind our experiences.

PARABLE OF THE RIVER

Once upon a time there was a small village on the edge of a river. The people there were good, and life in the village was good. One day a villager noticed a baby floating down the river. The villager quickly swam out to save the baby from drowning. The next day this same villager noticed two babies in the river. He called for help, and both babies were rescued from the swift waters. And the following day four babies were seen caught in the turbulent current. And then eight, then more, and still more!

The villagers organised themselves quickly, setting up watchtowers and training teams of swimmers who could resist the swift waters and rescue babies. Rescue squads were soon working 24 hours a day. And each day the number of helpless babies floating down the river increased. The villagers organised themselves efficiently. The rescue squads were now snatching many children each day. While not all the babies, now very numerous, could be saved, the villagers felt they were doing well to save as many as they could each day. Indeed, the village priest blessed them in their good work. And life in the village continued on that basis. One day, however, someone raised the question, 'But where are all these babies coming from? Let's organise a team to head upstream to find out who's throwing all of these babies into the river in the first place!'

Analysis of the river story

It is without question that the time to 'head up river' has come! What we remember in 'heading up river' is that our focus has to be on maternal and child health – not blame. It is apparent in many media reports that alcohol is being aggressively marketed at women, with significant consequences for women's health in general. Multi-agency professionals must respond proactively and continue to look at appropriate strategies to prevent ongoing harm to women and children.

PRACTITIONER PERSPECTIVES

Taking our lead from the *Parable of the River*, the authors have shared the question 'Where do we go from here?' with FASD advocates in different locations and fields. As acknowledged earlier, nations and cultures are at different stages in how FASD is seen and responded to, from advanced in some areas to non-existent and denial in others. So, for some of the contributions listed here, you will see that the hopes and desires for the future are more developed than others. Collectively, it does, however, show a genuine and significant need to ensure that individuals impacted by FASD attain the realistic hopes, desires and goals that they set for themselves. They qualify for the same rights as any individual living with a disability, and denying or compromising their rights should be challenged. Presentation of the following comments from those working or living with people with FASD seeks to demonstrate the worldwide impact of FASD.

Ireland

Joanna Fortune is a clinical psychotherapist specialising in Child and Adolescent Psychotherapy in Dublin, Ireland. Joanna approached an FASD educator when she had been working with an eight-year-old adopted child for some time. She had worked all the recommended theories and strategies around what was assumed to be attachment issues. After some time of little or no progress, Joanna decided to seek an assessment for FASD. Here Joanna reflects on her move from the traditional thinking on neurobehavioural conditions to consider the possibility of a pre-birth brain injury due to an alcohol-exposed pregnancy.

In my work with families of adopted children and children given care, there are some things that come up time and again; one is how alone they can feel in trying to get professional support for attachment challenges, and the other is how often attachment disorder and regulation disorder (also true of FASD) in this group of children gets diagnosed as something on the autism spectrum. These are not new problems in families, but they do require new thinking within the professional field to ensure that these children and these families get the help they need. Attachment can be healed and repaired, but this takes dedicated and focused work with an attachment specialist and needs to be done as joint parent–child work. This requires creativity and an openness to new ways of working therapeutically. Children with attachment, regulation or FAS disorders do not do well in non-directive play therapy, as not knowing what is expected of them can cause their anxiety to spike. The work within an attachment framework is to build the capacity for attachment in the child and work alongside the parent so that the attachment is transferred to the parent/carer and not the therapist. I have noticed in my work that along with the presence of an attachment and/or regulation disorder can be something else, something that attachment therapy alone cannot fix and something that also has its roots in early childhood trauma and neglect. FASD and PAE (prenatal alcohol effects) can manifest in a variety of ways, some of which will not emerge until the latency stage of development or even teenage years. FASD is often seen in a very medical model whereby a child is assessed for physical symptoms, and if those are not present, a diagnosis is not possible. In my work I have seen a small but significant number of cases where attachment work alone does not fully address the presenting behavioural and emotional issues. This tends to be with children who are aged 9–13 years and who had been doing relatively fine but are now seen to be regressing or are developmentally stuck and whose emotional development tends to be at a younger age. It is important to note that FASD and PAE may not emerge in physical symptoms but as psychological symptoms and/or mental illness as the child grows and develops, and as such it is very important that parents/ carers of children whose early childhood (those first two years) may not be fully understood are aware of what behaviours and symptoms may emerge at this later stage and how best to respond to this. We have very limited resources and few professionals specialising in this area, and often these children are diagnosed with attachment disorders and referred for attachment therapy, which can certainly help but is certainly not enough for these children. We need to understand more, to talk more and to encourage further writing, research and training in the area of FASD to raise awareness of these conditions and what the appropriate responses and treatments are.

Joanna Fortune, 15 November 2013

United States

Angelica Salinas is an outreach specialist working with a programme dedicated to children and families living with FASD in Wisconsin (USA).

FASD is a 100 per cent preventable disorder that affects so many lives, yet it is a disorder that we as a society know so little about. In order to prevent FASD, I believe the following needs to occur.

As a society we need to increase our awareness of how our own culture (whether it be racial culture, the culture of the community we live in, culture of our school, work and so forth) promotes the acceptance or non-acceptance of others, of alcohol and other drugs, of disability, of social economic status and so forth. As a society we need to understand the intended or unintended damage we do to women in the world by condemning them for being addicts and not having control in alcohol-friendly cultures. We as a society need to realise that the women we envision to be the problem – because they are court mandated into treatment – are average women, meaning they could be you or I. We as a society need to come together and educate each other, we need to educate doctors, nurses, social workers, allied health professionals, our neighbors, our children and our grandchildren, not just about the dangers of prenatal alcohol exposure but about forgiveness, compassion and reaching out and helping a stranger. Instead of casting negative images, thoughts and words, we need to see ourselves as that individual in that situation and be aware of how we would want and need to be treated in order to succeed.

Angellica Salinas, 13 November 2013

Michael L. Harris, in Minneapolis, Minnesota, is a trained psychologist and a foster parent. His reflection here demonstrates both 'a wish for FASD and "if I only had a magic wand…"'.

Yesterday, a wish for FASD occurred to me. I was attending a great foster care training and another participant had a coffee mug with a quote I hadn't heard but immediately liked:

> 'It would be so nice if something would make sense for a change'. (From *Alice in Wonderland*, 1951 Disney movie)

I've heard people say such things after they've fallen through the rabbit hole of FASD. Honestly, that basic sentiment has skipped through my own head a few times when I've found myself there:

- 'It doesn't make sense that I have to remind you to do this chore over and over and over.'

- 'It doesn't make sense why you're late coming back from the neighbour's house every night, even when wearing a watch.'

- 'It doesn't make sense to sneak into my closet at night to sleep instead of staying in your own nice bed.'

- 'It doesn't make sense for you to hide your completed homework instead of turning it in for credit.'

These have infinite variations, and any single one can be frustrating. Experience them multiple times over months, and you'll just feel angry, overwhelmed and burned out. So my wish is that these behaviours would make sense to people for a change. Then we could prevent burnout for caregivers and professionals, and promote harmony toward those with FASD. How nice that would be.

But here's the catch: every one of those FASD behaviours already makes perfect and total sense. The challenge that is we don't often remember or understand what causes those FASD behaviours. The above situations are accurately explained by memory problems, poor sense of time, sensory sensitivities and learning disabilities, respectively. And the root cause of them all? Prenatal alcohol exposure and trauma.

Do we remember this enough? Oh, if I only had a magic wand…

Michael L. Harris, MA, LP, SEP, 10 November 2013

Europe

Dr Diane Black of the European Alliance project based in the Netherlands has long championed the education issue of FASD within the European network. Her passion and drive is born personally from being a parent of adopted children living with FASD. Dr Black is a driving force behind biannual conferences in Europe.

In Europe, alcohol use during pregnancy has not been sufficiently addressed. We do not know how many women drink during pregnancy, nor do we know how many persons are affected by FASD; therefore, the European FASD Alliance has developed a vision document which includes the following goals:

- Everyone in Europe should know that there is no safe level for drinking during pregnancy.

- All medical professionals should be aware of the risks of drinking during pregnancy both on the fetus and the mother.

- Pregnant women should receive reliable information on the risks of drinking during pregnancy from their doctors and midwives.

- Pregnant women who are alcohol dependent should receive the necessary support to stop drinking during pregnancy.

- Required multiprofessional expertise for diagnosing FASD should be readily available in regional or national centres.

- Birth, foster or adoptive parents should receive the necessary support in raising children with FASD.

- Adults with FASD should have appropriate supported living and working situations.

In addition, we are lobbying the European Commission for action to support member states by supporting:

- the spread of information, including labelling of alcoholic beverage containers

- research to understand mechanisms and prevalence of FASD, and to develop evidence-based interventions for prevention, diagnosis and management

- the sharing of information and best practice among experts and policymakers.

These are our dreams, and what's more, we are working to make these dreams come true!

Diane Black, PhD, chair of the European FASD Alliance

Australia

Vicki Russell, CEO of NOFASD Australia, shares her thoughts about FASD and begins by acknowledging the 40-year journey to understanding how alcohol impacts the unborn.

The year 2013 marks the 40th anniversary of the rediscovery of fetal alcohol exposure and the naming of the fetal alcohol syndrome in 1973 by Jones and Smith. This event mobilised the prevention of alcohol in pregnancy by targeting 'alcoholic' women. Then as awareness grew of the broader spectrum of harms, the widening target group gathered in 'alcohol-dependent' women and 'alcohol-misusing' women. Now NOFASD Australia is encouraging all women who use alcohol during pregnancy to consider not drinking in pregnancy or breastfeeding, with the intention that an abstinence message needs to be conveyed to future parents to carefully consider alcohol in pregnancy planning.

FASD is not a registered disability in Australia, and yet the ever-increasing and high demand for a diagnosis is concurrent with a very limited number of 'qualified' FASD diagnosticians and waiting lists. The first national gathering of parents and carers took place in Brisbane, Queensland, in November 2013 and their common voice was one of anger, frustration and weariness at the failure of the service-provider sector and government to acknowledge their experience, to understand the condition and needs of the child, adolescent and adult. As one parent eloquently pointed out, 'knowing about FASD is not the same as understanding FASD'.

The previous government acknowledged FASD as a priority and allocated $20 million to a Commonwealth Action Plan on FASD. A change of government has created concern that the same level of commitment will not be matched. NOFASD Australia is the lead body representing individuals and families across Australia, and it is our fervent hope that a fair allocation of funds will support the much-needed services for families who live with FASD every day.

Vicki Russell, CEO, NOFASD Australia, 26 November 2013

England
Pip Williams is the founder of the European Birth Mums Network – FASD, and is a birth mother of two young men with FASD. She is also a board member of the European FASD Alliance.

There needs to be more awareness of FASD as well as the support needs of vulnerable women. We need early intervention for the mothers and we really need to start working with them at the beginning of their journey before it gets to the point when the children are experiencing challenging and damaging experiences. Due to the lack of meaningful support services for women with drug or alcohol misuse, domestic violence and trauma, their children often become part of the care system and the cycle of vulnerability repeats itself as the children age out of the fostering system and make their way in the world.

There needs to be a blanket public health message and full media coverage to bring awareness of FASD to the whole population. We need to start raising awareness early, perhaps even from Year 3 (ages eight to nine) when children start learning about healthy lifestyles and what is good to put in your body and what can cause harm. As the children age and receive health education lessons, they need to have clearer warnings about the risks of alcohol harm, unplanned pregnancies and FASD. We also need this issue to be brought to the attention of the boys and men, as this disability is not simply a woman's issue. Men have equal responsibility in the health of their child and may even be in the background causing some of the difficulties and dramas, and are often the ones who drink with their partners and bring alcohol into the home.

There has to be a consistent message of no blame and no shame. No woman wants to intentionally harm their baby. Misinformation is rampant, and often she doesn't know she is pregnant or realise the full extent of the harm that can happen from consuming alcohol. She needs support, the families need support and the children require a clear diagnosis and support. Too many doctors are giving sympathetic diagnoses, such as attention deficit hyperactivity disorder or autism, to spare the child, but these diagnoses don't help in the long run. We wouldn't treat diabetes with arthritic medications…and we shouldn't mislabel children. The mother goes to the doctor in search of answers and a diagnosis for her child, and too much time is being wasted worrying about the possible reactions and repercussions for the mother. They are there because they know that something is wrong with their child. Some of my birth mothers have asked doctors if they think their child's issues could be alcohol related and they are told no, even when later down the road it proves to be the case. We need clear, timely, honest diagnoses. We need to stop injustice being served and families being left unsupported.

Medical professionals…be brave and diagnose FASD. You're denying a child the right to the correct support to see them flourish and are compromising their future and the well-being of the family unit. There is much room for improvement.

Pip Williams, 29 January 2014

Scotland

Donna Ross is living in Scotland with her partner and her 13-year-old daughter. She is a full-time support practitioner for learners with special needs and runs an online support group for adults with FASD. Donna obtained her personal diagnosis of FAS at the age of 27, and whilst going through many of the challenges that adults with FASD face, she now lives a successful, independent, fulfilling life.

Doctors must recognise and understand that people with FAS can have complex health difficulties and they must not just assume they know what is going on with the individual but conduct proper examinations rather than relying on trial and error. If I have to deal with different doctors, I have to repeatedly explain my disability. This can put off people with FASD from going to see the doctor for treatment and cause further health problems.

People forget that because of the brain damage, people with FASD tend not to understand what is being asked of them. If they don't understand something, they need you to provide them with an explanation rather than simply repeating what you have just said. It is the lack of understanding that can cause them to make mistakes in life, get lower marks in education and feel as though they are failing. A simple tip in the classroom is, for example, if they are given an essay title that is difficult to understand, then you could use cue cards or a highlighter to identify the key words and concepts so that they don't miss the point of what you are asking them.

People with FASD can also find it hard to get motivated and deal with what most people find easy, for example time keeping. It can be really helpful if they have a watch that beeps to alert them that they must start getting organised to go out, or go somewhere or do something. There are lots of things that can stress people with FASD, so they may feel anxious a lot of the time. Help them to learn a variety of stress-reducing techniques, such as taking deep breaths, to help them stay calm. This is essential; otherwise, they may simply avoid tasks that make them feel stressful altogether and their everyday lives will become more challenging. Supporting them with everyday situations like bills, forms, appointments, shopping and so forth is vital, as there may be days where they need more support than others. So be there for those practical tasks.

Remember that every day is different, so what they seem to achieve one day they may find difficult the next day; therefore, patience is crucial as well as being prepared that this might happen. Always work to their strengths, praising their achievements no matter how small (e.g. washing, making a meal, dealing with travel or simply making their bed). Praise and encouragement helps increase their confidence and reminds them there are things that they can achieve just like everyone else.

Most importantly, always remember to try to understand them, even if they have challenging behaviour. They are often trying their best. I would say that the governments have to stop burying their heads in the sand and start addressing the issues of FASD to improve the lives and futures of so many people like me who have FASD and need a helping hand in order to thrive in our families and communities.

Donna Ross, 25 January 2014

PREVENTION STRATEGIES

FASD prevention and service-delivery work is complex on a number of levels. There are many different ideologies of how to approach 'prevention' of FASD with the many publications on the topic. One of the most acknowledged strategies in the prevention model was developed by Dr Anne Streissguth in her book *Fetal Alcohol Syndrome: A Guide for Families and Communities*, published in 1997. In this text Streissguth (1997) talks of the five Ps of prevention:

1. Public education.

2. Professional training.

3. Public policy.

4. Programmes and services.

5. Parent and citizen activism.

All physicians, allied health professionals and society at large are needed to participate in primary prevention efforts regardless of their medical or social role or responsibility. Training on brief intervention methods have demonstrated a level of success in reducing alcohol exposure in pregnancy. Holistic and joined-up approaches from medical and allied health personnel can include providing information about the dangers of drinking during pregnancy, screening women for risk of an alcohol-exposed pregnancy and referring women with alcohol problems for appropriate treatment and support. This can be best realised by providing clinical training and education as part of academic programmes to all multidisciplinary health professionals early in their careers. For such prevention strategies to work, they need to be advocated by political and policy providers. What such 'buy-in' looks like is detailed in the Edmonton Charter – a charter that was endorsed at the First International Conference on the Prevention of FASD in September 2013 and which summarises the latest evidence concerning FASD, calling on public health agents and governments globally to act on both prevention and the public health crisis that FASD presents.

Strategies aimed at preventing alcohol-exposed pregnancies include the following:

- *Universal prevention efforts* aim to educate the public about the dangers of alcohol use during pregnancy. Prevention strategies include warning labels on alcoholic beverages, public service announcements and mass media campaigns.

- *Selective prevention interventions* target individuals or a subgroup of the population who are at increased risk for having an alcohol-exposed pregnancy – that is, all women of childbearing age who drink alcohol. Prevention strategies include screening women for alcohol use and providing brief interventions for women at risk for an alcohol-exposed pregnancy. Alcohol screening instruments include the TWEAK, T-ACE, CAGE and AUDIT, which are freely available for such interventions.

- *Indicated prevention interventions* target women at highest risk for giving birth to a child with FASD, including women who have previously given birth to a child with FASD or a woman who has a known history of alcohol abuse or dependence. Prevention strategies include alcohol treatment and measures to prevent pregnancy (Hankin 2002).

IMPLICATIONS FOR THE ALCOHOL INDUSTRY

There has been a push in recent years to be clear about what is going into the foods that we consume. A clear example of this is the horsemeat scandal of 2013, where the finding of 'undeclared' horse meat in frozen beef burgers by the Food Safety Authority of Ireland led to a scandal that quicly spread throughout Europe and to further questions about food regulation. Other examples centre on the obesity crisis and questions about the amounts of fat, salt and sugar in processed foods. People intently check food labels to ensure that their foods do not contain any ingredients that are considered unsafe or harmful to health, including ingredients which may be harmful to people with nut allergies or milk intolerance. Yet, alcohol products are not approached with the same vigour, and there are relatively few people who would perceive alcohol to be a poison or toxin. Alcohol labels do not clearly identify the contents or place standardised labels which state that the contents are toxic or dangerous to unborn children. Labelling which follows the protocols on cigarettes and states that 'this toxin has the ability to harm the developing fetus' is available only in some parts of the world, namely the US and France. This is clearly one area of public policy that needs addressing with urgency if prevention of harm to the unborn is to be taken seriously. The implications of not seeking to prevent FASD are significant both in terms of human suffering and public health service budgets.

IMPLICATIONS FOR SOCIAL SERVICES
AND CHILD WELFARE AGENCIES

When the behaviours of people with FASD become too much for the family home, individuals may be placed into the state care system at great cost to the taxpayer. Social services can provide for individuals who cannot live independently, and treatment is provided for those who develop addiction habits. There is a myriad of services to address the mental health needs of young people and adults whose brain is not functioning correctly due to an injury they received before birth – FASD. But what is often glaringly missing in these 'responses' is an acceptance or awareness that the individual may have a brain-based injury preventing compliance with what society expects as the 'norm'. Existing interventions in many situations of the caring profession are not tailored to the needs of FASD, resulting in this child with a neurobehavioural profile not having their needs met in care placements. Where parents, carers and professionals incorporate approaches which accommodate the brain injury, the potential for the child to achieve success in their life is greatly increased. It is true on some level that the child welfare services are just beginning to 'wake up' to FASD within its system. It needs to be followed by clear policy directives on training, respite and assessment/diagnostic services if we are to see meaningful change in meeting the needs of these young people living with FASD.

The majority of admissions into state residential and foster care systems are due to dysfunction within the home of drug and alcohol misuse by parents, leading to neglect and general welfare concerns by social workers. Such circumstances raise the possibility that children from within such environments are at high risk of having been exposed to alcohol while in utero, and thus carry an element of neurobehavioural dysfunction in their presentation. It is for that reason that screening for FASD should be a high priority in all child welfare cases on admission to care systems. FASD is not just a medical issue – it is a social issue that will prevail throughout the child's entire life. Social workers on the frontlines need to proactively recognise this disability and seek a diagnosis that can help the individual to navigate the ever-increasing complexity of their journey through life.

Sadly, FASD is not included in most social work undergraduate training programmes of education. Social work is a key profession for identifying and supporting those affected by the detrimental effects of alcohol in pregnancy, yet the professional training of social workers rarely equips them with the knowledge and skills required to make the correct interventions. In truth, the lack of training and education in the profession of social work often can lead to conflict, with the adoptive/foster parent seeking help for the child in their care. Raising children with FASD is a significant challenge for a caregiver – one that many carers may not be fully prepared for prior to accepting a child living with FASD. Where foster or adoptive parents can be trained together with social workers, this can greatly reduce the potential for conflict in seeking to meet the needs of caring for a child with a neurobehavioural profile. Evidence suggests that children in foster and adoption care have elevated levels of behavioural issues related to FASD. It is often the case that the social worker holds the keys to respite care and specific service provision, such as behaviour management interventions, speech and language therapy and so forth, to assist the child in their developmental needs. Where the carer understands the disability of FASD and the social worker has had no education, conflict of caring ideals and principles can be severely compromised, leading to strained relationships between key providers of interventions.

Evidence also would suggest that not seeing the disability of FASD in the foster care and indeed the adoption service can lead to placement disruption and complete breakdown. Sadly, the term 're-homing' has begun to emerge in the US, where adoption cases have completely broken down, most often due to out-of-control neurobehavioural reasons beyond the ability of the adoptive parents. It is somewhat disturbing to consider that the term 're-homing', which is more commonly used in animal welfare, is attributed to children coming from international adoptions. Adoptive parents do not necessarily have the supports and knowledge on FASD to manage such challenges within the home. Caregivers want to create opportunities for success and celebrate the strengths of these children living with FASD. This can be achieved if they are supported in their role of caregiving and not consumed in an adversarial process of having to campaign for very basic needs. If this non-adversarial role between provider and caregiver can be achieved, then the potential for stable placements is greatly enhanced, obviating the disruptions and breakdowns that happen too commonly in many care systems.

IMPLICATIONS FOR PUBLIC HEALTH POLICY

FASD is not recognised as a disability in many parts of the world. This needs to be rectified by governmental policy directives in health, thus creating the proper access and development of services to accommodate this disability within society. The burden of FASD permeates all societies around the world, and the lifelong implications of failing to prevent this preventable disability are enormous. In many places, FASD diagnostic services are being carried out in isolated and individual settings. A singular diagnostic physician working in isolation, and without a multidisciplinary support structure for the child or adult, can be very troublesome for the parent, carer or professional in responding to a new diagnosis. Think of it like this: An individual who receives a diagnosis for a serious illness has a collective of individuals and services assigned to assist with the management of the illness. Take, for example, the diagnosis of cancer. A consultant oncologist will most likely break the bad news to the individual. The oncologist is then likely to refer the individual back to the family physician to develop a case management strategy for the individual. This can involve the family physician engaging up to 10 or 15 professionals, all of whom will play a key role in ensuring the individual with the diagnosis of cancer gets the best possible care.

The majority of diagnoses under the FASD umbrella term have no visible features, which significantly adds to the challenge of providing appropriate diagnostic and early intervention services. Revising the cancer analogy, however, it is also likely that the individual will have no visible features of this destructive invasive illness, yet they will receive every possible service that the state and community can provide. If FASD was embedded in a mainstream disability, such as autism, Asperger syndrome or Down syndrome, then society would be more likely to respond more appropriately, correctly and sensitively to an FASD diagnosis.

A diagnosis can have very little meaningful effect if it is not followed up by appropriate services and interventions. The majority of responses by existing specialist practitioners, who are already working in the disability and special education services, does not allow for the neurobehavioural profile associated with FASD. Most interventions and treatments in an FASD diagnosis are non-pharmacological and usually involve changing the approach and the environment of the child or adult. It requires that individuals in the life of that child or adult see the primary disability of a non-organic brain injury and accommodate their needs; therefore, having clear national and regional diagnostic services that embody the principle of multidisciplinary assessment and diagnostic process can greatly aid the flow of care planning to those on the front line of caring provision. Families and caregivers require services to be available throughout the lifespan. A diagnosis will be of limited value if it is not backed up by skilled and trained professionals delivering services when they are needed.

Diagnostic services are weak in many corners of the world; however, both the US and Canada have forged the way in this particular skill. Public health bodies seeking to develop their diagnostic policy or strategy can learn a great deal from these pioneering countries. Collaboration across international boundaries in tackling the public health challenge of FASD is greatly encouraged. Furthermore, there is no need to reinvent the wheel when it comes to prevention strategies. These countries mentioned also have a wealth of experience and enacted policies which could greatly inform the public health needs of many countries in the developed world.

IMPLICATIONS FOR UNDERGRADUATE AND POSTGRADUATE EDUCATION

This book has demonstrated that the complex and multiple needs of individuals living with FASD cannot be addressed by a single professional. A full assessment team is made up of many different professionals, all of whom have a role to play in meeting the varied and complex needs that may be present in a child or adult who has experienced an alcohol-exposed pregnancy. The assessment process of FASD should be delivered only by highly skilled and trained professionals who are fully familiar with the complexities and the variance of FASD presentations in children and adults.

There is a need for FASD modules to be included in undergraduate education as a crucial component of meeting the holistic challenge of seeing FASD addressed in our communities. Those people studying to work with children both in the social services system and the education system should have a particular emphasis placed on the need to understand and become knowledgeable about FASD. It is the responsibility of professionals once qualified and out in the 'field' to campaign for FASD education to be provided in line with their continuing professional development requirements.

Professionals should also be taught that pregnancy is a key motivator for women to seek change in their alcohol or illicit drug use. Having professionals trained to capitalise on this moment to motivate change may significantly aid the prevention of FASD within our communities.

It is also recommended that the training of professionals be delivered by properly trained facilitators typically from the same profession being trained (e.g. social workers trained by a social worker). Professionals need to comply with ethical codes of professional practice and avoid any aspect of stigma or blame in their work with women and birth mothers. This can be achieved only if allied health professionals are provided with the skills to impart this information in a non-judgemental, supportive and empowering manner.

What pregnant women want from health professionals is honest and truthful advice about alcohol. This can be achieved by allied health professionals adhering to the collective and most accepted scientific view that there is no known safe level of alcohol in pregnancy. Any alcohol consumed while pregnant is deemed to be risky. All pregnant women who drink heavily are placing the unborn child at a higher risk of the full effects of learning disability, behavioural problems and the physical effects of PAE.

Even when a pregnant woman drinks moderately or lightly, there remains a risk of affecting the delicate balance of brain circuitry development, resulting in potential behavioural and learning challenges in the child post-birth. FASD is not a disability of 'blame' for those birth mothers who have a child with brain injury from an alcohol-exposed pregnancy; rather, it is one of education and empowerment through knowledge that alcohol poses risks to their unborn child.

Universal FASD education should be provided at all levels within communities, and this education needs to be continuous and systematic – not just a 'flash in the pan' of leaflet production left in community health centres in the hope that people will read it. Prevention of this disability is possible; however, each woman's reason for drinking is different. There needs to be full consideration of the complex nature of why some women consume alcohol while pregnant, and there needs to be mechanisms in place to help them make informed decisions at the time they are ready to make some changes in their lifestyles.

Public health education needs to work long and hard at filling the knowledge gap between what is known in terms of scientific evidence and how that can translate meaningfully to men and women within local communities. The fact that large numbers of children are conceived every year exposed to a toxin that can devastate their lives, and that there is no proactive framework to warn the general public of the dangers and prevent it, is unconscionable.

SUMMARY OF KEY MESSAGES FROM RESEARCH

Key messages from research confirm the following points:

- Alcohol consumed during pregnancy increases the risk of alcohol-related birth defects, including growth deficiencies, facial abnormalities, CNS impairment, behavioural disorders and impaired intellectual development.

- No amount of alcohol consumption can be considered safe during any trimester in pregnancy.

- Alcohol can damage a fetus at any stage of pregnancy. Damage can occur in the earliest weeks of pregnancy, even before a woman knows that she is pregnant.

- The cognitive deficits and behavioural problems resulting from PAE are lifelong and incurable. Interventions can help to mitigate the effects on daily living.

- Alcohol-related birth defects and CNS damage is completely preventable.

For these reasons, the following applies:

- A pregnant woman should choose not to drink alcohol during pregnancy.

- A pregnant woman who has already consumed alcohol during her pregnancy should stop in order to minimise further risk.

- A woman who is considering becoming pregnant should abstain from alcohol.

- Recognising that nearly half of all births are unplanned, women of childbearing age should consult their physician and take steps to reduce the possibility of PAE.

- Health professionals should inquire routinely about alcohol consumption by women of childbearing age, inform them of the risks of alcohol consumption during pregnancy and advise them not to drink alcohol during pregnancy.

- Adhering to healthy pregnancy advice on folic acid, choline and vitamins may be counterproductive and may mitigate the positive effects of such actions if alcohol is consumed simultaneously.

Chapter 7

FASD – A PUBLIC HEALTH CHALLENGE FOR ALL

This book may have been an eye-opener and indeed an upsetting read for some people. What the evidence is telling us to date is that FASD is the leading cause of brain injury in childhood today and is cited as the leading cause of developmental disability in the Western world. The impact on our public health policy is enormous for the individual, family, community and on a societal level.

Over the past 40 years, the Western world has known the devastating impact that alcohol can cause on the unborn child while at its most vulnerable life stage in utero. Although the evidence has been around since biblical times, actions centre on the reactive 'picking up the pieces' approach, which treats the symptoms and behaviours of fetal alcohol exposure rather than focusing more widely on prevention strategies. Global and universal public health awareness of this devastating disability has been largely absent within public health policy responses. Even in 2014, the response to alcohol in pregnancy is a very ad-hoc and piecemeal approach in many corners of the world. Reliable diagnostic procedures have been available in certain parts of the developed world for over a decade but are not being developed in the vast majority of countries. Children, adolescents and adults with FASD, as well as their families, require that society open its mind to this devastating disability that prevails at all levels within community and society.

The cost to society to support children and adults affected by PAE is enormous, with a heavy psychosocial impact on the family. In community terms, we increasingly expend monetary and physical resources just dealing with the *symptoms* of the problem instead of tackling the root cause. The question of not screening for fetal alcohol exposure is even more questionable when we consider the economic health costs of FASD in our societies (yearly estimates in local currencies are US 6.2 billion, Canada 5.3 billion, UK 2.2 billion, Australia 66 million and New Zealand 16 million). Although the cost burden to society is staggering, we must not forget the human suffering that lies behind such figures. The individuals living with FASD and struggling for acceptance and understanding from a society that does not recognise the disability is the real tragedy. More awareness, understanding and acceptance of this pervasive disability would lead to earlier diagnosis and better societal interventions to enable and empower those people who need it most.

Within the past few years, the US, Canada and, more recently, Australia have grasped the nettle, by ensuring holistic and joined-up thinking on the prevention, diagnosis and management of the disability in their societies. In fact, August 2013 saw Australia make one of the biggest funding announcements of recent times when the Australian Minister for Mental Health outlined a four-year plan and funding of $20 million Australian dollars to address the issue of FASD in Australia. Whilst Australia has a long way to go, the fact that government bodies are involved is a very positive sign. In comparison, Ireland, with a population of 4.4 million people and a confirmed research statistic of drinking in pregnancy at 80 per cent, launched its very first all-Ireland public health information in September 2013 to warn of the risk of drinking in pregnancy, but no funding was identified for tackling the issues of preventing or managing FASD in its society.

At the same time, the First International Conference on FASD, held in the Canadian city of Edmonton with some 700 delegates from 35 countries, created the world's first charter on FASD prevention. This charter includes a direct call to international governments and policymakers to address FASD in a systematic and coordinated manner. A key statement of the charter is as follows: 'The cause of FASD is known and preventable. Broad-based policy initiatives and actions at different levels of every society are urgently needed to encourage abstinence from alcohol during pregnancy.'

Although the US and Canada have developed public health responses, European countries tend to make isolated statements in the absence of any real policy directives seeking to educate and change perceptions of alcohol use in pregnancy. Ironically, many European states have excellent public health information on antenatal care. Ireland is rated very highly in

Europe for its campaigns on folic acid and healthy pregnancy information, but with an absence of alcohol risk warnings. Coupled with an absence of national diagnostic guidelines in most European countries, misclassification or misdiagnosis is potentially leading to a lot of FASD cases remaining unrecognised, thus creating unprecedented levels of secondary disabilities and human suffering. This can be easily rectified by creating diagnostic services with wrap-around care planning for lifelong interventions to meet the varying needs as and when they present.

Ultimately, this book was written in order to show that the child or adult living with FASD need not have a trajectory of failed life chances. Indeed, the opposite is true. Individuals who are supported with early intervention, and who are supported by informed and proactive multi-agency professionals, and have families and educational workers who are adapting the environment to accommodate the individual, will see the greatest life outcomes. Many adults with FASD would say that there is a lot of improvement to services needed, and while this is true, many more of them are completing their compulsory education and some are going to universities. More than ever, they are successfully engaging in work, living independently and raising families. Many of them are making their mark in sports, writing, public speaking, photography, traditional crafts, animal care and child care, and have battled along with their families to make that possible in their lives. It is time to make everything less of a battle and more about equity in terms of rights to public health services so that more children will be protected from alcohol exposure in the womb, and those that are prenatally exposed will be able to achieve the goals that much of society may take for granted.

> Although there is no 'cure' for the brain damage induced by prenatal alcohol…exposure, we can indeed influence a child's life for the better by redirecting him into a regulated, smooth and mutually interactive dance with the people that matter most in his life.
>
> (Chasnoff 2011)

AFTERWORD – MAKING PROGRESS IN THE FUTURE

In 2000 I was appointed Chair of the US National Task Force on FAS/FAE by the US secretary of Health and in the following year as Co-Chair of the FASD Center for Excellence. One of my most eye-opening experiences in these positions was to participate in 14 Town Hall meetings held across the United States in 2002–2003, where individuals with FASD, their families and caregivers, service providers, researchers, policy makers, and community leaders were invited to share their stories and discuss issues important for individuals with FASD. We heard from over 200 parents and caregivers, over 30 individuals with FASD, and 160 professionals and community leaders. Several common themes emerged including numerous gaps in multiple systems of care, lack of knowledge and services within the educational, legal, and health professions, and lack of appropriate diagnostic services. People expressed a need for effective prevention strategies, increased services for women with a substance abuse problem, education about FASD at all levels, better diagnostic services, services for dealing with FASD in every system of care, recognition of FASD as a disability, supportive housing, and enactment of adoption disclosure laws concerning prenatal alcohol exposure. Since those meetings, certainly progress has been made, but the needs expressed then are still pervasive now.

Progress has been made in terms of education on many fronts. Years ago, when I told people what I did, I had to explain about FAS, now almost everyone says 'oh, fetal alcohol syndrome.' They may not always get it right, or understand the wider FASD spectrum, but at least they are aware of FAS. Similarly, one can always tell when some character on TV or in a movie becomes pregnant, because she stops drinking. Professional organizations internationally are also recognizing FASD.

For example, in the US in 2011 the American Academy of Pediatrics in coordination with the Interagency Coordinating Committee of FASD, the National Institute on Alcohol Abuse and Alcoholism, and the Centers for Disease Control and Prevention issued a consensus statement that advocated for the broad education of the public and health professionals about behavioral problems associated with 'Alcohol Related Neurodevelopmental Disorder'(www.niaaa.nih.gov/sites/default/files/ARNDConferenceConsensusStatementBooklet_Complete.pdf). Similarly, in 2012, The American Bar Association passed a resolution urging 'attorneys and judges,…bar associations, and law school clinical programs to help identify and respond effectively to FASD…through training…' They even urged the passage of laws that 'acknowledge and treat' issues related to FASD (American Bar Association 2012). The Canadian Bar Association went even further, resolving to 'urge all levels of government to allocate additional resources for alternatives to the current practice of criminalizing individuals with FASD' (Canadian Bar Association, 2012).

In Europe the European Fetal Alcohol Spectrum Disorders Alliance (EUFASD) and the European Alcohol Policy Alliance (Eurocare) in collaboration with the Local Health Authority of Treviso, Italy, have proposed to launch an awareness campaign on alcohol and pregnancy in 2014. This programme will involve a number of institutions, nongovernmental organisations, and associations throughout the European countries belonging to the World Health Organisation, with the aim of sharing objectives, materials and resources to develop an integrated communication campaign. This proposal of a European coordinated and systematic action will be supported by sponsors and partners to develop a campaign of quality, supported by an efficient evaluation system. Europe is still within an 'infancy' stage of its approach to FASD. There is a paucity of diagnostic services and inter-professional skills in responding to the psychosocial aspects of support to those living with FASD and their caregivers. The need for governmental buy-in is essential, with its public health agencies developing structural acceptance of FASD as a leading cause of disability with European society.

Another recent significant development was the decision to include Neurobehavioral Disorder Associated with Prenatal Alcohol Exposure (ND-PAE) in the Appendix of the DSM-5, as a condition in need of further study. Importantly, the DSM-5 includes the possibility of diagnosing '315.8 Other specified neurodevelopmental disorder' using 'associated with prenatal alcohol' as a reason for that disorder. We are now waiting to see how FASD will be treated in the revision of the International Classification of Diseases (ICD) codes, as this could have a major impact in how FASD is treated throughout the world. Progress has been slow, but progress has been made.

Diagnostic progress has also been made. Although there is currently no universal set of criteria for the diagnosis of the disorders included under the rubric of FASD, I see more agreement than disagreements in this area. It would really be great if in the near future there was a consensus conference to develop a set of criteria for the various conditions under the spectrum that could be applied universally. There certainly has been an increase in the number of facilities offering diagnostic services for FASD. For example, over 700 professionals have completed a course on the 4-Digit code technique, for diagnosis of FASD across the spectrum. Additionally, dysmorphologists have provided training videos on more traditional diagnostic techniques, and numerous live physician trainings have been held throughout the world. Most recently, advances in facial imaging and computerized analysis techniques have been applied experimentally with some success in diagnosing FAS and perhaps even being able to help determine those without all of the facial features of FAS, but who may be at risk for behavioral problems.

A few final points I would like to mention. Usually when one hears about a putative teratogenic agent, or an agent that might harm a child, it is simply avoided. Alcohol evokes another response altogether. I find it an uncomfortable truth that even infinitely small amounts of substances such as BPA, an agent with hormone-like properties used to harden plastic, causes public outcry when present in baby bottles, yet some women still ask how much alcohol is safe to consume during pregnancy. Headlines appear stating that low or moderate levels of alcohol are safe, and in fact, may even be beneficial. I am always baffled by this, as the science certainly indicates that heavy prenatal alcohol exposure is harmful, and that a host of factors such as the timing or exposure, the dose, pattern of drinking, an individuals' genetic makeup, nutritional status, all enter into the equation of whether a child will be affected or not.

For any individual it would be all but impossible to determine a threshold of effect. So obviously, the safest choice is to simply avoid alcohol. We also need to eliminate any stigma attached to FASD. Women need better information about the consequences of prenatal alcohol exposure and those in the health professions regularly need to ask women about their drinking behavior, the same way they do about smoking. Women with an alcohol problem need access to services and treatment, not finger pointing if we are going to prevent FASD.

Finally, I was among the first to demonstrate that prenatal alcohol exposure could cause behavioral effects in the offspring and I have long advocated that alcohol was a behavioral teratogen. However, I also recognize that not every behavioral problem in a child of a woman who consumed alcohol during her pregnancy is the result of that alcohol exposure. We need to be realistic in what we call an alcohol-related neurodevelopment disorder (ARND) or a neurodevelopmental disorder as a result of prenatal exposure to alcohol (ND-PAE), taking into account other possible causes, such as genetics and other environmental factors. There are certainly enough individuals who truly have cognitive and behavioral issues related to prenatal alcohol exposure that we cannot overwhelm the systems of care by suggesting that all cognitive and behavioral problems in an individual with any prenatal alcohol exposure has an FASD. Until more data are collected better describing the behavioral phenotype(s) seen following such exposure we need to take a realistic assessment of the problem or we risk being not taken seriously.

Edward P. Riley, PhD
Distinguished Professor.
Director, Center for Behavioral Technology
San Diego State University.

APPENDIX: SLEEP ASSESSMENT

Sleep habits	Yes, we already do this	Yes, we think this would help	Not right now, that won't work
Your child maintains a regular wake-up and bedtime routine every day, including weekends (maximum deviation of 1 hour).			
Your child is exposed to sunshine (or some other form of bright light) during the day.			
Your child's day has a balance of activity and rest.			
Your child takes short naps only in the early afternoon.			
As a general rule, your child does only quiet activities in the last hour prior to going to bed.			
Your child eats/drinks only light, healthy foods/beverages before going to bed. Your child does not eat food during the night.			
Your child's TV, DVD and computer game (screen) time is limited.			
You have a regular bedtime routine with your child, including story time (see also social stories).			
You recognise your child's cue for tiredness.			
You put your child to bed while drowsy but still awake in the same place where they sleep all night.			
Your child is in bed by 7, 8 or 9 pm depending on his/her age and needs.			

- Regularity (of both sleep times and mealtimes) encourages your child's body cycles to be coordinated. Maintaining a regular wake-up time is most important for our sleep/wake cycle.

- Exposing children to sunshine during the day, after their wake time, particularly in the morning, may help them sleep better at night. Bright light helps the body to produce melatonin (a natural sleep hormone) that promotes better sleep and mood.

- The planning of daily activities is important. Children benefit from structure and routine as well as balanced patterns of both activity and rest during the day and night. Recognising the relationship between daytime activity and sleep promotion is important.

- Daytime naps should be geared around the child's age and development. We recommend that a nap not be taken after 3 pm.

- Calming activities include well-structured routine behaviours, such as quiet baths, listening to stories and/or lullabies. Vigorous activities may stimulate your child, and afterwards it may take them several hours to relax. Having a bath before bedtime with a bright light, shallow water and many toys can make the bath exciting rather than calming. Storytelling could have a calming influence, but unfamiliar stories or books with loud sounds (e.g. animal noises) may be stimulating. A bath with deeper water, dim lights and soft, familiar songs may calm.

- Overeating before bedtime can interfere with your child's sleep. Light, healthy snacks, such as cheese and crackers (protein and carbohydrates, like a diabetic snack) or oatmeal, are recommended. Avoid food and drinks with caffeine (e.g. hot chocolate, chocolate cookies, energy drinks and cola) 4–6 hours before sleep. Allowing regular night mealtimes quickly teaches the body to wake up during the night because it needs to 'be fed'. If required, your child may drink water.

- Screen time creates an excess of stimuli and should be avoided at night; however, a favourite and familiar DVD following dinner may be calming for some children, although it could result in over-stimulation for others.

- A series of regular activities, carried out in the same sequence (e.g. changing into pyjamas, brushing teeth, going to the toilet and turning off the lights), allows the body to prepare for sleep. Your bedtime routines should not be longer than 30 minutes. Encourage your child to complete part of the bedtime routine independently (e.g. let your child turn off the lights), as this strengthens his or her sense of control and independence.

- When children become tired, they exhibit some of their bedtime-routine activities (e.g. rubbing eyes, taking off socks). When you recognise that your child is getting tired, help them to get fully ready for sleep. Even slightly dozing off in the late afternoon or at night time can affect quality of sleep during the night.

- Take your child to bed when he or she is awake, and then leave the room before they fall asleep; otherwise, your child will constantly associate falling asleep with your presence.

- Children need different amounts of sleep depending on their age and individual needs. We recommend that children between the ages of five and ten years go to bed no later than 9 pm.

(Adapted from Jan *et al.* 2008, 2010)

BIBLIOGRAPHY

Abraham, V. (2005) *An Investigation into the Needs of Parents with FASD*. Masters thesis, University of Northern British Columbia, Canada.

Adams, C. M., Kodituwakku, P. W., Hay, A., Vilyoen D., May, P. A. (2001) 'Patterns of cognitive-motor development in children with fetal alcohol syndrome from a community in South Africa.' *Alcoholism: Clinical and Experimental Research 25*, 557–562.

Ainsworth, M. D. (1963) 'The Development of Infant–Mother Interaction Among the Ganda.' In B. M. Foss (ed.) *Determinants of Infant Behavior* (pp.67–104). New York: Wiley.

Ainsworth, M. D., Belhar, M., Waters, E. and Wall, S. (1978) *Patterns of Attachment: A Psychological Study of the Strange Situation*. Hillsdale, NJ: Lawrence Erlbaum Associates.

American Academy of Pediatrics. Committee on Substance Abuse and Committee on Children with Disabilities (2000) 'Fetal alcohol syndrome and alcohol-related neurodevelopment disorders.' *Pediatrics 106*, 2, 358–361.

American Bar Association. Resolution 112B (2012). Available at www.americanbar. org/content/dam/aba/administrative/mental_physical_disability/Resolution_112B. authcheckdam.pdf, accessed on 8 July 2014.

American Psychiatric Association (1994) *Diagnostic and Statistical Manual of Mental Disorders* (4th ed.). Washington, DC: American Psychiatric Association.

American Psychiatric Association (2013) *Diagnostic and Statistical Manual of Mental Disorders* (5th ed.). Arlington, VA: American Psychiatric Publishing.

Astley, S. J. and Clarren, S. K. (1999) *Diagnostic Guide for Fetal Alcohol Syndrome and Related Conditions: The 4-Digit Diagnostic Code* (2nd ed.) Seattle, WA: University of Washington Publication Services.

Berlin, L. J., Cassidy, J. and Appleyard, K. (2008) 'The Influence of Early Attachments on Other Relationships.' In J. Cassidy and P. R. Shaver (eds) *Handbook of Attachment: Theory, Research and Clinical Applications* (pp.333–347). New York and London: Guilford Press.

Bertrand, J., Floyd, R. L., Weber, M. K., O'Connor, M. *et al.* (2004) *National Task Force on Fetal Alcohol Syndrome and Fetal Alcohol Effects: Guidelines for Referral and Diagnosis*. Atlanta, GA: Centers for Disease Control and Prevention.

Blackburn, C. (2009) *Building Bridges with Understanding Project: Foetal Alcohol Spectrum Disorders: Focus on Strategies*. Worcestershire Sunfield Research Institute, Worcestershire County Council. Available at www.worcestershire.gov.uk/cms/pdf/2010-05%20 54126%20FASD%20Strategy%20doc%20AMENDED%20v1.pdf, accessed on 17 December 2013.

Bowlby, J. (1951) *Maternal Care and Mental Health*. Monograph. Geneva: World Health Organization.

Bowlby, J. (1953) *Child Care and the Growth of Love*. London: Penguin Books.

Burd, L., Cohen, C., Shaw, R. and Norris, J. (2011) 'A court team model for care of young children in foster care: the role of prenatal alcohol exposure and fetal alcohol spectrum disorders.' *Journal of Psychiatry and Law 39*, 179–191.

Buxton, B. (2005) *Damaged Angels*. Cambridge, MA: Da Capo Press.

Canadian Bar Association. Resolution 10-02-A, Fetal Alcohol Spectrum Disorder in the Criminal Justice System. Available at www.cba.org/ABC/resolutions/pdf/10-02-A.pdf, accessed on 8 July 2014.

Catterick, M. (2013) 'If I was in Charge…': The Experiences of Adolescents and Adults with Fetal Alcohol Spectrum Disorder and the Implications for Service Delivery. Unpublished dissertation.

Centers for Disease Control (CDC) (2004) *Fetal Alcohol Spectrum Disorder: Competency Based Curriculum Guide for Medical and Allied Health Education and Practice*. Atlanta, GA: CDC.

Chasnoff, I. (2011) *The Mystery of Risk: Drugs, Alcohol, Pregnancy, and the Vulnerable Child*. Chicago, IL: NTI Upstream.

Chudley, A. E., Conry, J., Cook, J. L., Loock, C., Rosales, T. and LeBlanc, N. (2005) 'Public Health Agency of Canada's National Advisory on Fetal Alcohol Spectrum Disorder: Canadian guidelines for diagnosing.' *Canadian Medical Association Journal 172*, SI–121.

Clark, E., Lutje, J., Minnes, P. and Oullette-Kuntz, H. (2004) 'Secondary disabilities among adults with fetal alcohol spectrum disorder in British Columbia.' *Journal of FAS International 2*, e13.

Coles, C. (1994) 'Critical periods for prenatal alcohol exposure.' *Alcohol Health Research World 18*, 1, 22–29.

Coles, C. D. (1997) 'A comparison of children affected by prenatal alcohol exposure and attention deficit, hyperactivity disorder.' *Alcoholism: Clinical and Experimental Research 9*, 454–460.

Connor, P. D., Sampson, P. D., Bookstein, F. L., Barr, H. M., Steissguth, A. P. (2000) 'Direct and indirect effects of prenatal alcohol damage on executive function.' *Developmental Neuropsychology 18*, 331–354.

Debolt, D. (2009) *Creating Touchstones: Support to Adults with FASD*. Report from Lakeland Centre for FASD. Available at http://lcfasd.com/wp-content/uploads/2013/05/Creating-Touchstones-Support-to-Adults-with-Fetal-Alcohol-Spectrum-Disorder.pdf, accessed on 13 December 2013.

Densmore, R. (2011) *FASD Relationships: What I Have Learned about Fetal Alcohol Spectrum Disorder*. Salmon Arm: Dory Spirit Books Ltd.

Denys, K., Ramussen, C. and Henneveld, D. (2011) 'The effectiveness of a community based intervention for parents with FASD.' *Community Mental Health Journal 47*, 2, 209–219.

Duquette, C. and Orders, S. (2013) 'On fitting a triangle into a circle: a study on employment outcomes of adults with FASD who attended postsecondary institutions.' *International Journal of Alcohol and Drug Research 2*, 3, 27–36.

Egerton, J. (2009) *Foetal Alcohol Spectrum Disorders: Information Sheets*. Worcestershire: Sunfield Research Institute.

Fagerlund, A., Autti-Ramo, I., Kalland, M., Santtila, P. *et al.* (2012) 'Adaptive behaviour in children and adolescents with fetal alcohol spectrum disorders: a comparison with specific learning disability and typical development.' *European Child and Adolescent Psychiatry 21*, 221–231.

Fuchs, D., Burnside, L., Marchenski, S., Mudry, A. and De Riviere, L. (2008) *Economic Impact of Children in Care with FASD. Phase 1: Cost of Children in Care with FASD in Manitoba*. Ottawa, ON: Centre of Excellence for Child Welfare.

Grant, T., Huggins, J., Connor, P. and Streissguth, A. (2005) 'Quality of life and psychosocial profile among young women with fetal alcohol spectrum disorders.' *Community Mental Health Journal 40*, 6, 499–511.

Hankin, J. R. (2002) 'Fetal alcohol syndrome prevention research.' *Alcohol Research & Health 26*, 1, 58–65.

Herrick, K., Hudson, L. and Burd, L. (2011) 'The elephant in the cradle: fetal alcohol spectrum disorder.' *Zero to Three Journal 31*, 44–50.

Hoyme, H. E., May, P. A., Kalberg, W. O., Kodituwakku, P., Gossage, J. P. *et al.* (2005) 'A practical clinical approach to diagnosis of fetal alcohol spectrum disorders: clarification of the 1996 Institute of Medicine criteria.' *Paediatrics 115*, 39–47.

Hughes, D. (2012) *Parenting a Child with Emotional and Behavioural Difficulties*. London: BAAF.

Human Rights Act (1998) Chapter 42. London: The Stationery Office.

Hutson, J. R., Stade, B., Lehotay, D. C., Collier, C. P. *et al.* (2012) 'Folic acid transport to the human fetus is decreased in pregnancies with chronic alcohol exposure.' *PLoS One 7*, 5, e38057.

Jan, J. E., Asante, K. O., Conry, J. L., Fast, D. K. *et al.* (2010) 'Sleep health issues for children with FASD: clinical considerations.' *International Journal of Pediatrics*, 14 July, doi:10.1155/2010/639048.

Jan, J. E., Owens, J. A., Weiss, M. D., Johnson, K. P. *et al.* (2008) 'Sleep hygiene for children with neurodevelopmental disabilities.' *Pediatrics 122*, 6, 1343–1350.

Jones, K. L. and Smith, D. W. (1973) 'Recognition of the fetal alcohol syndrome in early infancy.' *Lancet 2*, 836, 999–1001.

Jonsson, E., Dennett, L. and Littlejohn, G. (eds) (2009) *FASD Across the Lifespan*. Edmonton, Alberta: IHE Publications.

Kapp, F. M. E. and O'Malley, K. D. (2002) *Watch for the Rainbows: True Stories for Educators and Other Caregivers of Children with Fetal Alcohol Spectrum Disorders* (revised 1st ed.). Calgary: Frances Kapp Education.

Kodituwakku, P. W. (2007) 'Defining the behavioural phenotype in children with fetal alcohol spectrum disorders.' *Neuroscience and Behavioural Reviews 31*, 192–201.

Kodituwakku, P. W., Handmaker, N. S., Cutler, S. K., Weathersby, E. K., Handmaker, S. D. (1995) 'Specific impairments in self-regulation in children exposed to alcohol prenatally.' *Alcoholism: Clinical and Experimental Research 19*, 1558–1564.

Kodituwakku, P. W., Handmaker, N. S., Kalberg, W. and May, P. A. (2001) 'The effects of prenatal alcohol exposure on executive functioning.' *Alcohol Research and Health 25*, 192–198.

Koren, G., Zelner, I. and Nash, K. (2014) 'Foetal alcohol spectrum disorder: identifying the neurobehavioral phenotype and effective interventions.' *Current Opinion in Psychiatry 27*, 2, 98–104.

LaDue, R. A. (2002) *A Practical Native American Guide for Caregivers, Adolescents and Adults with FAS and Alcohol Related Conditions.* Rockville: Indian Health Service.

Lemoine, P., Harousseau, H., Borteyru, J. B. and Menuet, J. C. (1968) 'Les enfants de parents alcooliques: anomalies observées, à propos de 127 cas.' *Quest Medical 21*, 476–482.

Lutke, J. and Antrobus, T. (2004) *Fighting for a Future.* Available at www.fasdconnections.ca/HTMLobj-1807/fighting_for_a_future.pdf, accessed on 21 April 2013.

Machiavelli, N. (2003) *The Prince.* London: Penguin.

Main, M. and Solomon, J. (1986) 'Discovery of an Insecure Disoriented Attachment Pattern: Procedures, Findings and Implications for the Classification of Behaviour.' In T. Brazelton and M. Youngman (eds) *Affective Development in Infancy* (pp.121–160). Norwood, NJ: Ablex.

Malbin, D. V. (2002) *Fetal Alcohol Spectrum Disorders: Trying Differently Rather Than Harder.* Portland, OR: Tectrice Inc.

Malbin, D. V. (2008) *Fetal Alcohol Spectrum Disorders: A Collection of Information for Parents and Professionals* (2nd ed.). Portland, OR: FASCETS Inc.

Maslow, A. H. (1943) 'A theory of human motivation.' *Psychological Review 50*, 370–396.

Mattson, S. N. and Riley, E. P. (1998) 'A review of the neurobehavioral deficits in children with fetal alcohol syndrome or prenatal exposure to alcohol.' *Alcoholism: Clinical and Experimental Research 22*, 279–294.

Mattson, S. N., Riley, E. P., Gramling, L., Delis, D. C. and Jones, K. L. (1997) 'Heavy prenatal alcohol exposure with or without physical features of fetal alcohol syndrome leads to IQ deficits.' *Journal of Paediatrics 131*, 718–721.

Mattson, S. N., Riley, E. P., Gramling, L., Delis, D. C., Jones, K. L. (1998) 'Neuropsychological comparison of alcohol exposed children with or without the physical features of fetal alcohol syndrome.' *Neuropsychology 12*, 146–153.

Mattson, S. N., Goodman, A. M., Caine, C., Delis, D. C. and Riley, E. P. (1999) 'Executive functioning in children with heavy prenatal alcohol exposure.' *Alcoholism: Clinical and Experimental Research 23*, 1808–1815.

May, P., Fiorentino, D., Coriale, G., Kalberg, W. O., Hoyme, H. E. *et al.* (2006) 'Epidemiology of FASD in a province in Italy: prevalence of characteristics of children in a random sample of schools.' *Alcoholism Research and Health 30*, 1562–1575.

McCarthy, F. P., O'Keefe, L. M., Khashan, A. S., North, R. A. *et al.* (2013) 'Association between maternal alcohol consumption in early pregnancy and pregnancy outcomes.' *Obstetrics & Gynecology 122*, 4, 733–734.

McCreight, B. (1997) *Recognizing and Managing Children with Fetal Alcohol Syndrome/Fetal Alcohol Effects: A Guidebook.* Washington, DC: CWLA Press.

McGee, C. L. and Riley, E. P. (2006) 'Brain imaging and FASD.' *Annali dell'istituto Superiore di Sanità 42*, 46–52.

Moore, K. L., Persaud, T. V. N., Torchia, M. G. (2011) *The Developing Human: Clinically Orientated Embryology.* Oxford: Elsevier.

Mercer, J. (2006) *Understanding Attachment: Parenting, Childcare, and Emotional Development.* Westport, CT: Praeger Publishers.

Merrick, J. and Kandel, I. (2007) 'Fetal alcohol syndrome and suicide: a review.' *International Journal on Disability and Human Development 6*, 3, 237–239.

Merrick, J., Merrick, E., Morad, M. and Kandel, I. (2006) 'Fetal alcohol syndrome and its long-term effects.' *Minerva Pediatrica 58*, 3, 211–218.

NOFAS UK (nd) *Alcohol and Pregnancy: Information for Midwives.* London: MENCAP/NOFAS UK. Available at www.nofas-uk.org, accessed on 7 January 2014.

O'Connor, M. J. and Paley, B. (2009) 'Psychiatric conditions associated with prenatal alcohol exposure.' *Developmental Disabilities Research Reviews 15*, 225–234.

Olson, H., Feldman, J. J., Streisguth, A. P. *et al.* (1998) 'Neuropsychological deficits in adolescents with fetal alcohol syndrome: clinical findings.' *Alcoholism: Clinical and Experimental Research 22*, 9, 1998–2012.

O'Malley, K. D. (ed.) (2007) *ADHD and Fetal Alcohol Spectrum Disorders.* New York: Nova Science Publishers.

Pakkenberg, B. and Gundersen, H. J. (1997) 'Neocortical neuron number in humans: effect of sex and age.' *Journal of Comprehensive Neurology 384*, 312–320.

Popova, S., Lange, S., Burd, L. and Rehm, J. (2013) 'Canadian children and youth in care: the cost of fetal alcohol spectrum disorder.' *Child & Youth Forum. Journal of Research and Practice in Children's Service.* Available at http://link.springer.com/article/10.1007%2Fs10566-013-9226-x/fulltext.html, accessed on 30 November 2013.

Ragsdale, J. (2006) *Interventions and Supports for Adults with Fetal Alcohol Spectrum Disorder: An Integrative and Interpretive Review.* Masters thesis, University of North British Columbia, BC, Canada.

Rasmussen, C. (2005) 'Executive functioning and working memory in fetal alcohol spectrum disorder.' *Alcoholism: Clinical and Experimental Research 29*, 1359–1367.

Rasmussen, C. and Wyper, K. (2007) 'Decision making, executive functioning and risky behavior in adolescents with prenatal alcohol exposure.' *International Journal on Disability and Human Development 6*, 4, 405–416.

Riley, E. P. and McGee, C. L. (2005) 'Fetal alcohol spectrum disorders: an overview with emphasis on changes in brain and behavior.' *Experimental Biology and Medicine 230*, 357–365.

Riley, E. P., McGee, C. L. and Sowell, E. R. (2004) 'Teratogenic effects of alcohol: a decade of brain imaging.' *American Journal of Medical Genetics Part C. Seminars in Medical Genetics 127C*, 35–41.

Rutman, D. and Van Bibber, M. (2010) 'Parenting with fetal alcohol spectrum disorder.' *International Journal of Mental Health and Addiction.* Available at http://fasd.alberta.ca/documents/Parenting-with-FASD.pdf, accessed on 30 January 2013.

Rutman, D., La Berge, C. and Wheway, C. (2002) *Adults Living with FAS/FAE: Experiences and Support Issues in British Columbia.* Victoria, BC: FASD Support Network BC and University of Victoria School of Social Work.

Salmon, J. V. and Buetow, S. A. (2012) 'An exploration of the experiences and perspectives of New Zealanders with FASD.' *Journal of Popular Therapy and Clinical Pharmacology 19*, 1, e41–e50.

Samuels, M. A. and Ropper, A. H. (2009) *Adams and Victor's Principles of Neurology* (9th ed.). New York: McGraw-Hill.

Schemenauer, C. A. (2011) *Support to Improve the Lives of Adults with FASD: An Ethnographic Study of a Mentorship Program.* Masters thesis, University of Saskatchewan, Saskatoon, Canada.

Schonfeld, A.M., Mattson, S.N., Lang, A.R., Delis, D.C. and Riley, E.P. (2001) 'Verbal and nonverbal fluency in children with heavy prenatal alcohol exposure.' *Journal of Studies on Alcohol 62,* 239–246.

Shelov, S. and Remer, T. (2009) *Caring for Your Baby and Young Child: Birth to Age 5* (5th ed.). New York: Bantam.

Spadoni, A. D., McGee, C. L., Fryer, S. L. and Riley, E. P. (2007) 'Neuroimaging and fetal alcohol spectrum disorders.' *Neuroscience Biobehavioral Reviews 31,* 239–245.

Spohr, H. (1996) 'Fetal Alcohol Syndrome in Adolescence: Long-Term Perspective of Children Diagnosed in Infancy.' In H. Spohr and H. Steinhaussen (eds) *Alcohol, Pregnancy, and the Developing Child* (pp.207–226). Cambridge: Cambridge University Press.

Spohr, H., Willms, J. and Steinhausen, H. C. (2007) 'Fetal alcohol spectrum disorders in young adulthood.' *Journal of Pediatrics 150,* 2, 175–179.

Steinberg, L. (2005) *The Ten Basic Principles of Good Parenting.* New York: Simon and Schuster.

Stratton, K., Howe, C. and Battaglia, F. (eds) (1996) *Fetal Alcohol Syndrome: Diagnosis, Epidemiology, Prevention and Treatment. Institute of Medicine.* Washington, DC: National Academy Press.

Streissguth, A. P. (1997) *Fetal Alcohol Syndrome: A Guide for Families and Communities.* Baltimore, MD: Paul H. Brookes.

Streissguth, A. P. and O'Malley, K. (2000) 'Neuropsychiatry implications and long term consequences of fetal alcohol spectrum disorders.' *Seminars in Clinical Neuropsychiatry 5,* 177–190.

Streissguth, A. P., Aase, J. M., Clarren, S. K., Randels, S. P., LaDue, R. A., Smith, D. F. (1991) 'Fetal alcohol syndrome in adolescents and adults.' *Journal of American Medical Association 265,* 1961–1967.

Streissguth, A. P., Barr, H. M., Kogan, J. and Bookstein, F. L. (1996) *Understanding the Occurrence of Secondary Disabilities in Clients with Fetal Alcohol Syndrome (FAS) and Fetal Alcohol Effects (FAE).* Final Report to the Centers for Disease Control and Prevention (CDC). Tech Report No 96-06. Seattle, WA: University of Washington, Fetal Alcohol and Drug Unit.

Streissguth, A. P., Bookstein, F., Barr, H. M., Sampson, P. D., O'Malley, K. and Young, J. K. (2004) 'Risk factors for adverse life outcomes in fetal alcohol syndrome and fetal alcohol effects.' *Journal of Developmental & Behavioral Pediatrics 25,* 4, 225–228.

Sullivan, W. C. (1899) 'A note on the influence of maternal inebriety on the offspring.' *Journal of Mental Science 45,* 489–503.

Thomas, N. (2008) *When Love is Not Enough: A Guide to Parenting with RAD – Reactive Attachment Disorder.* Glenwood Springs: Families By Design.

Victorian Order of Nurses (VON) (2005) *Let's Talk FASD: Parent Driven Strategies in Caring for Children with FASD.* Ottawa, Ontario: VON Canada.

ADDITIONAL RESOURCES

There are many international resources available. A selection of groups which include a number of geographical areas are given below.

United Kingdom
NOFAS UK
www.nofas-uk.org
FASD Network
www.fasdnetwork.org
FAS Aware
www.fasaware.co.uk
FASD Scotland
www.fasdscotland.com
FASD Ireland
www.fasd.ie

Europe
European Birth Mother Network – FASD
(based in UK but European-wide support)
www.eurobmsn.org
European FASD Alliance
www.eufasd.org
SAF France
www.saffrance.com
FAS World Deutschland
www.fasworld.eu
Società Italiana sulla Sindrome Feto-Alcolica
www.sifasd.it
FAS Foreningen (Sweden)
www.fasforeningen.nu

USA
NOFAS
www.nofas.org
MOFAS
www.mofas.org
FASD Elephant
www.FASDElephant.com

Canada
CANFASD
www.canfasd.ca
POPFASD
www.fasdoutreach.ca
FASLINK
www.faslink.org

Australia
NOFASD Australia
www.nofasd.org.au
Russell Family Fetal Alcohol Disorders Association
www.rffada.org

SUBJECT INDEX

AUTHOR INDEX